WHAT AMERICAN CULTURAL LEADERS
ARE SAYING ABOUT

In the Lion's Den . . .

"Nina Shea has performed an invaluable service for Christians around the world in writing *In the Lion's Den*. Her meticulous documentation of the moving drama of the tragic persecution of Christians around the globe will arouse the conscience of the Christians who read it. *In the Lion's Den* is a powerful weapon to motivate Christians to work diligently and to pray passionately for an end to the atrocities being visited upon their fellow Christians."

> DR. RICHARD D. LAND, PRESIDENT
> The Ethics and Religious Liberty Commission
> Southern Baptist Convention

"Perhaps no issue in our time is more pressing than that of the brutal and intense persecution and murder of tens of thousands of our fellow Christians abroad. Nina Shea and the Puebla Program on Religious Freedom are on the forefront of keeping track of this persecution. *In the Lion's Den* gives a helpful overview of the problem. Every Christian in America should read this short book and then get involved!"

> D. JAMES KENNEDY, PH.D.
> Senior Minister
> Coral Ridge Presbyterian Church

"This primer should be in every Christian household. The sufferings of many Christians in the world today are unspeakable. They cry out to our hearts. The least we can do is open ourselves to learn of them, and unite with them in prayer."

> MICHAEL NOVAK
> George Frederick Jewett Scholar in Religion
> and Public Policy
> American Enterprise Institute for
> Public Policy Research

"*In the Lion's Den* is a disturbing account of Christian persecution in today's world. It calls attention to one of the most gruesome—but most neglected—stories of contemporary suffering. We ought to take seriously the Biblical injunction to "bear one another's burden." And so we ought to do far more than we have done to act against the evils being perpetrated against Christians around the world. This book offers so many practical things we can do."

WILLIAM J. BENNETT
Author of *The Book of Virtues*

"Too few Christians know, and act on, the fact that we live in the greatest century of persecution in Christian history. This book, a masterpiece of concise research on one of the most urgent human rights issues of our time, ought to shake the churches out of their ignorance and complacency."

GEORGE WEIGEL
Senior Fellow
Ethics and Public Policy Center

"Few Christians are aware, too few Christians seem to care, that ours is the century of the martyrs. It is happening right now. Please read *In the Lion's Den,* and then pray about what God wants you to do."

THE REV. RICHARD JOHN NEUHAUS
President
Religion and Public Life

"For too long, Americans have been told to keep quiet about the persecution and killing of Christians in Saudi Arabia and Sudan. We have been told not to rock the boat in China when Christians in "house churches" are hunted down. "Quiet diplomacy" has not worked; it has only made matters worse. Aleksandr Solzhenitsyn advised us, when we cried out against the violation of fundamental human rights in the Soviet Union, not to fear the charge we were meddling. "Meddle!" he said. Nina Shea and Freedom House are to be commended for their brave witness. *In the Lion's Den* is must reading for every American who cares about our first freedom."

GARY L. BAUER
President
Family Research Council

This enormously timely book is exactly what the public debate needs— a passionate argument that is well-documented and fully supported by facts. But the real beauty is that it's about one of the great stories of our time and it's a story that almost nobody knows. Shea deserves our thanks.

PEGGY NOONAN
Author

In the Lion's Den contains vital information for those involved in human rights advocacy and for Christians concerned about their fellow believers overseas. Today, Christians are being persecuted in record numbers while the world remains silent. This book helps break that silence.

> REPRESENTATIVE FRANK WOLF (R-VA)
> U.S. House of Representatives

"Inhuman persecution of Christians in other countries, and more subtle persecution in America are rampant. It must be exposed and stopped. May God use this book to inform and cause men and women of conscience to do something about it."

> WILLIAM R. BRIGHT
> President
> Campus Crusade for Christ International

"We must no longer be silent to the plight of thousands of Christians around the world suffering and dying because of matters of conscience and faith. This must be a time of a new solidarity of consciences by Christians around the world. Every Christian should prayerfully consider *In the Lion's Den* and then seek ways to come to the aid of those now persecuted for the sake of the Gospel."

> CARL A. ANDERSON
> Vice President for Public Policy
> Knights of Columbus

"The tragic fact is that Christians have become the special targets of religious persecution in the world today. *In the Lion's Den* should be required reading for all American Christians. This book not only gives the facts but suggests practical, achievable steps for stopping these reigns of terror. As the Statement of Conscience of the National Association states, "it is our responsibility, and that of the government that represents us, to do everything we can to secure the blessings of religious liberty to all those suffering from religious persecution."

> DON ARGUE
> President
> National Association of Evangelicals

"Religious liberty is among the most basic of human rights. Yet the magnitude of persecution, torture and isolation of Christians around the world is both stunning and unconscionable. The West must not be ignorant about the atrocities being done to Christians or those of any faith in Asia, Africa and the Middle East. Nor can we be silent. We must expose persecution to the light of day and be the champion of free people, free markets and free elections. The world is looking to us to show moral leadership. I urge people to read this penetrating Freedom House primer and heed its call to action."

STEVE FORBES
Honorary Chairman
Americans for Hope, Growth and Opportunity

"Most Americans are not aware of the widespread violations of Christians' human rights in many parts of the world. For a full briefing on what is happening, read *In the Lion's Den*. It will tell you why Christians are being persecuted, how they are being persecuted, and who is doing it. This valuable book also tells us how we can help stop the attack on Christians abroad."

JEANE KIRKPATRICK
Former U.S. Ambassador to the United Nations

"*In the Lion's Den* is an excellent publication on the persecuted church. It highlights the tragic fact that more Christians have died because of their faith in this country than in the first nineteen centuries after the birth of Christ."

REPRESENTATIVE TONY HALL (D-OH)
United States House of Representatives

"It's tragic that most Americans don't even know that believers are still being persecuted today throughout the world. During the Cold War everyone was very aware of Christians being oppressed in the Soviet Union and the Eastern Bloc countries. But when the Iron Curtain fell, many Christians thought that was essentially the end of it. In fact, the incredible brutality against Christians in many other parts of the world has multiplied along with the growth of Christian communities. We must focus great prayer and resources on our brothers and sisters still being held. *In the Lion's Den* is essential reading for us to learn what is occurring and how we can respond."

JOSH MCDOWELL
Josh McDowell Ministries

"*In the Lion's Den* can help us experience the healthy growth taking place today—broadening awareness all of us need concerning the suffering and persecution being borne by our brothers and sisters around the world."

JACK W. HAYFORD, D. LITT.
Senior Pastor
The Church On The Way
Van Nuys, California

"Very few Americans are aware of the atrocities experienced by Christians around the world, those Christians who dare to practice their religious convictions. And, far too few Christians address this issue by speaking against such barbaric and inhuman conditions. In *In the Lion's Den*, Nina Shea provides a stirring glimpse of specific examples of global Christian persecution. Hopefully, this synoptic evidence will provoke the participation of American Christians to stem the tide in areas where such prevalence exists. The reading of this book is a must for Christians and non-Christians alike."

JOSEPH ESSARD JACKSON, D.MIN
Executive Director
Church of God Black Ministries Department
Cleveland, Tennessee

in the
LION'S
DEN

FOREWORD BY CHUCK COLSON

in the LION'S DEN

A Shocking Account of Persecution and Martyrdom of Christians Today & How We Should Respond

NINA SHEA

AFTERWORD BY RAVI ZACHARIAS

BROADMAN & HOLMAN PUBLISHERS

NASHVILLE, TENNESSEE

Published by Broadman & Holman Publishers, Nashville, Tennessee
Acquisitions & Development Editor: Matt Jacobson
Interior Design: Desktop Miracles, Addison, Texas

4263-57
0-8054-6357-7

Dewey Decimal Classification: 248.5
Subject Heading: Witness Bearing / Persecution
Library of Congress Card Catalog Number: 96-49176

Unless otherwise noted, Scripture quotations are from the Holy Bible, New International Version, copyright © 1973, 1978, 1984 by International Bible Society. Other Scripture are marked NRSV, New Revised Standard Version of the Bible, copyright © 1989 by the Division of Christian Education of the National Council of Churches of Christ in the United States of America, used by permission, all rights reserved.

Library of Congress Cataloging-in-Publication Data
Shea, Nina
    In the lion's den : persecuted Christians and what the Western Church
can do about it / Nina Shea.
        p.   cm.
    ISBN 0-8054-6357-7 (pbk.)
    1. Christian martyrs. 2. Persecution. 3. Church history. I. Title.
BR1601.2.S46   1997
272'.9—dc21   96-49176
                                                                      CIP

00 01 5

TO MY HUSBAND

Adam Meyerson

Acknowledgments

This report was compiled with research and writing
by Kim A. Lawton.

Contents

Foreword

BY CHUCK COLSON

WHEN YOU HEAR ABOUT CHRISTIANS being martyred for their faith, do you think of biblical figures such as Stephen or John the Baptist?

If you do, you're out of date by a couple thousand years.

In fact, more Christians have been martyred for their faith in this century alone than in the previous nineteen centuries combined. More than followers of any other faith, Christians around the world are suffering brutal persecution. Volume upon volume of irrefutable, documented evidence continues to surface, revealing horrifying atrocities increasingly being committed against those who dare to follow Jesus Christ.

The examples are heartbreakingly plentiful. The list of afflictions reads like an alphabet of cruelty: amputation, bombing, crucifixion, displacement, flogging, kidnapping, murder, prison, rape, slavery, and torture. The sheer dimensions of the problem are mind-boggling.

In Sudan, the Muslim government has made it a crime to convert to Christianity—a policy enforced brutally. As the Khartoum government troops move south, where most Christians live, believers are given three options: convert, flee, or be killed. Thousands of children have been snatched from Christian families and many sold as slaves to buyers in Sudan, Libya, and other Islamic countries. Thousands of women have been raped; others have been sold as servants or concubines. Reports tell of men being crucified.

Not long ago in Sudan a mother sent her nine-year-old son, Peter, to the market to buy tomatoes. But Peter never made it. Police officers of the Muslim government grabbed Peter, threw him into a truck, and drove him to a concentration camp where officials beat the boy brutally until he renounced Christ and converted to Islam.

But Sudan is not the only persecuting country. In Pakistan Christians have been driven from their villages by Muslim mobs, their possessions looted, their homes and churches destroyed. Christian evangelization is outlawed by a blasphemy law that prohibits speaking against the prophet Mohammed, punishable by death. A twelve-year-old child was recently sentenced to death and freed only by international pressure.

In Egypt both converts and ethnic Coptic Christians are being persecuted, their businesses looted and their churches burned.

In Iran four prominent evangelical pastors have been abducted and assassinated in the last few years. Many Christians have been arrested and tortured; others have lost homes, jobs, and businesses. Armenian and Assyrian Christian schools have been closed or taken over by Muslims.

Since the Gulf War, police in Saudi Arabia have arrested and abused hundreds of Christians—believers whose only crime was engaging in religious activities. Citizens are paid a bounty of three thousand dollars for exposing a home Bible study class.

In Vietnam Christians are subject to arrest, threats, and confiscation of their homes.

In North Korea Christians are forced to meet secretly in private homes, and they have no access to Bibles or religious materials.

In China up to one hundred million Christians risk their lives daily by defying government orders banning free worship.

All of this—and much more—goes on as the leading superpower of the world, the United States, does little in response, even though federal laws require that the Immigration and Naturalization Service (INS) investigate claims of religious persecution. Instead of helping those suffering people, the U.S. government often makes their plight worse. For example, when Christians fleeing from religiously oppressive regimes contact U.S. embassies, the INS often sends them back home, denying their plight. The INS literally delivers these persecuted believers up like lambs to the slaughter.

The State Department knows religious persecution is going on in communist and Islamic countries, but because of other foreign policy concerns, they choose to look the other way. (For years many

American political leaders refused to acknowledge religious persecution by communist governments; these leaders only grudgingly accepted the horror of the Russian gulag after Solzhenitsyn's books were smuggled out.)

Christians in the United States must work to change this—and they need to turn on the heat until *real* change comes about. They have every reason to take the lead on this because more than 350 years ago the Puritans journeyed to these shores in search of religious freedom. Sixty years later the Quakers settled Philadelphia as a haven for persecuted sects. Even in this century Armenian and Assyrian Christians fleeing Turkey were welcomed by the U.S. with open arms.

Furthermore, the right to worship God according to one's conscience is recognized in our founding documents as a basic, inalienable human right. So if Christians in America stand by and do nothing as their brothers and sisters in other parts of the world suffer, they are abandoning the proudest heritage they have as Americans. They are also abandoning their birthright as Christians.

Christian citizens need to do something when the U.S. government refuses to safeguard religious liberties around the world. It is time for Christians to use pulpits and publications to cry out in defense of fellow believers. It is time to write to representatives in Washington, D.C., demanding reforms in INS policy and calling for the protection of persecuted Christians as a top priority when the U.S. negotiates with other countries. We need to try to influence foreign service policy to require any country receiving assistance from the United States to maintain basic standards of human rights and religious liberties.

Christians also need to keep the suffering church in prayer. Suffering believers in faraway lands will never forget our prayers and public expressions of concern for them. I think of the Soviet dissident and poet Irena Ratushinskaya, who spent seven years imprisoned in the former Soviet Union's notorious gulag; she told me that she endured deprivation and all kinds of stress because she knew that people around the world were praying for her.

I wonder what God would do if all His people were on their knees begging for mercy for their persecuted brethren. At the very least, a praying church in this country would show the church world-wide that American Christians are not self-indulgent, uncaring people who do not care about our brothers and sisters in Christ.

The challenge is to make a commitment to remember perse-cuted Christians abroad and to maintain this commitment day in and day out. Many things work against that kind of commitment. Plagued by the problem of the issue du jour, Americans can easily lose a sense of reality in the parade of issues broadcast on televi-sion night after night. But with a crisis of this magnitude—blatant persecution—the consciences of Christians must be seared.

May God grant that Christians who are so comfortable in freedom never consider prayer too great an effort, stay informed, and speak out in defense of those who are willing to pay the ultimate price for their faith.

It's a Crime
to Be Christian

MILLIONS OF AMERICAN CHRISTIANS pray in their churches each week, oblivious to the fact that Christians in many parts of the world suffer brutal torture, arrest, imprisonment, and even death—their homes and communities laid waste—for no other reason than that they are Christians. The shocking, untold story of our time is that more Christians have died this century simply for being Christians than in the first nineteen centuries after the birth of Christ. They have been persecuted and martyred before an unknowing, indifferent world and a largely silent Christian community. And as their suffering intensifies, our silence becomes more stark.

Eleven countries where Christians are currently enduring great religious persecution are profiled in the following pages: China, Sudan, Pakistan, North Korea, Saudi Arabia, Vietnam, Egypt, Nigeria, Cuba, Laos, and Uzbekistan. Although these countries contain but a small sample of the Christians victimized throughout the world for their faith, they represent some of the worst—if not *the* worst—oppressors of Christianity in the world. They evidence a worldwide trend of anti-Christian persecution based on two political ideologies—communism and militant Islam. Around the globe, these two ideologies have consistently oppressed Christians, as well as other independent groups and individuals. While there are cases of persecution of Christian minorities by Hindus, Buddhists, and even by other dominant Christian groups, it is anti-Christian persecution by communism and militant Islam that, because of their global sweep and virulence, poses the greatest threat.

It is important to understand the distinction between persecution and discrimination or bigotry. The most egregious human rights atrocities are being committed against Christians living in communist and militant Islamic societies solely because of their religious beliefs and activities. The atrocities include torture, enslavement, rape, imprisonment, forcible separation of children from parents, killings, and massacres—abuses that threaten the very survival of entire Christian communities, many of which have existed for hundreds or even a thousand years; abuses that frequently thwart the ability of others to follow their consciences toward Christ.

In some cases—such as in China and Sudan—it is the regime that is the oppressor. In others, including Pakistan and Egypt, societal forces are at work, while the government—out of weakness—acquiesces, failing to stop the persecution despite well-organized assaults or known instigators. In most cases, Christians are minorities within the society, but not in all—Christians in Cuba and Nigeria form the majority but remain oppressed.

The rights of Christians and other groups to practice their religion freely—irrespective of the culture and customs of an area, or a Christian community's minority status—is universally recognized in the Universal Declaration of Human Rights and numerous other international treaties and instruments. In other words, the United Nations' world body has agreed that Christians have fundamental rights to express their Christianity, even in non-Christian parts of the world. The most specific of these documents is the United Nations' *Declaration on the Elimination of All Forms of Intolerance and of Discrimination Based on Religion or Belief*. This declaration guarantees the right of Christians and others to worship freely, as well as the right to teach religion, write and disseminate religious publications, designate religious leaders, communicate with coreligionists at home and abroad, solicit and receive charitable contributions, and educate children in religion and morality according to parents' wishes. In the country discussions that follow, these rights are honored primarily in the breach.

Many readers will be familiar with claims of bias and hostility directed at Christians here in America. However objectionable the treatment of Christians and their views in the United States, this bigotry pales in comparison to the atrocities suffered by Christians in many communist and Islamic nations. The following catalog lists cruelties that have occurred over the past year.

- In China, three Protestant evangelicals, including Zhang Xiuju, a thirty-six-year-old woman, were beaten to death by police in connection with a vicious government crackdown on the independent house-church movement. Many more were arrested and joined thousands of other Christians in China's religious gulag. Chinese police are currently circulating an arrest warrant that bears the names of three thousand evangelical preachers. They are among as many as one hundred million Christians in China who are forced to risk their lives daily by defying communist government orders that ban free worship.

- An Islamic court in Kuwait declared Robert Hussein an "apostate" because he converted to Christianity after learning about it as a student at Temple University in Philadelphia.[1] The court stripped him of his rights to his family and property, suggesting that he be put to death. He fled into exile for fear of his life.

- Seven Trappist monks, the oldest an eighty-two-year-old doctor, were taken hostage by Algeria's Armed Islamic Group. Two months later their throats were slit by their terrorist captors. In total, nineteen Catholic clerics were assassinated in Algeria over four years.

- As the militant Muslim government of Sudan prosecutes its religious war against the Christian southern part of the country, thousands of Christian children have been captured from their families and sold at open-air slave markets for as little as fifteen dollars per child. They were taken north to countries in the Middle East or other parts of Sudan where they must work as domestic slaves, field hands, soldier-slaves or concubines for their Muslim masters.

- Mohammad Bagher Yusefi, a prominent young pastor with the Assemblies of God Church in Iran, was found dead under suspicious circumstances. He is the fourth prominent figure in Iran's tiny Christian community to die a probable martyr's death in the past three years. In 1994 Iran's militant Islamic president delivered a fiery sermon, declaring that "there is no

3

longer validity to other religions," and that "Iran and the entire Muslim world must adopt the Prophet and Jihad (holy war) as a model."[2] Two weeks later Rev. Haik Hovsepian-Mehr, leader of the Iranian Assemblies of God Church, was kidnapped, tortured, and murdered by unknown assailants. His successor as head of the Iranian Protestant Council, Presbyterian minister Tateos Machaellian, vanished and was found brutally murdered a few months later. The beloved pastor, Mahedi Dibaj, was found murdered soon after.

- A Catholic priest in Vietnam is halfway through a twenty-year prison term imposed because his popular religious order organized adult catechism classes. Ten other members of his order are also serving prison time after being sentenced in the same trial.

The men, women, and children cited above are among millions of Christians currently facing ferocious campaigns against them because of their religious beliefs. This persecution is a global problem. It is prevalent in the remnant Communist countries, including North Korea, Vietnam, Cuba, Laos, and China, home to one-fifth of the world's population. In parts of the Islamic world—in countries such as Sudan, Saudi Arabia, Iran, Pakistan, Egypt, and Uzbekistan—the persecution of Christians is on the rise as advances are made by a militantly politicized strain of Islam where extremists, distorting Islam's tolerant values, seek to use religion to grab state power. It is no accident that the places where Christians are most severely persecuted are also among the countries rated as being among the least free in Freedom House's annual survey, *Freedom in the World*.

Christians are the chief victims of this religious persecution around the world today. In many countries they suffer not just discrimination or bigotry but torture, imprisonment, and the ultimate test of faith, martyrdom. It is difficult for Westerners to imagine the savageries encountered by these Christians—or the spiritual commitment necessary to endure persecution and death for the sake of faith.

It should be hardly surprising that Western Christians have had difficulty empathizing with their suffering brothers and sisters of faith. Most Westerners are shocked to learn that Christians are still being persecuted throughout the world. Few in the West feel comfortable speaking about these human rights atrocities. But intolerant and authoritarian regimes everywhere are well aware of the punishment meted out to Christians for the simple act of being Christian.

Christians are targeted by ruthless dictators who demand total power and control, intolerant of those who believe in the Supreme Being—the transcendent God—or in the inherent dignity of all persons created in God's image. They serve as scapegoats for societies that aim to vent, foment, and popularize hatred of the West and, most specifically, the United States. They are demonized by militant and xenophobic Islamist movements seeking to capture the soul of a historically tolerant Islamic faith. By their faith, Christians pose inherent threats to those regimes that rely on bribes and threats to maintain power.

If Christians are being persecuted and even martyred on such a massive scale throughout the world today, why don't we know about it?

Richard Land, president of the Christian Life Commission of the Southern Baptist Convention, recently attested before Congress to some of the reasons why we Americans have ignored the increasingly grim fates of brave Christians abroad:

> The persecution of Christians in various parts of the world has not been a high profile item on America's agenda. . . . First, too often people in the West, peering through the selective prism of Christian history in the West, reflexively think of Christians as persecutors rather than the persecuted. [Further], an increasingly secularized West and its leadership elite tend to be indifferent and often uncomprehending of a spiritual worldview which endures persecution and death for the sake of belief.[3]

With rare exception, our political leaders have been unaware of or else they turned a blind eye to this unfolding tragedy. Since the end of the cold war, American political leaders have generally shown indifference—even hostility—to Christians abroad, rarely taking religious oppression against them into account when devising foreign policy. Our presidents in recent years have repeatedly spoken about human rights abuses against vulnerable minorities throughout the world, but they have failed to address the persecution of Christians, even though it is among the most pervasive international human rights problems. Why?

In the fundamental matter of religious freedom, the United States is forfeiting its leadership. Before leaving for his diplomatic post in China in early 1996, U.S. Ambassador Jim Sasser was never briefed by the State Department about the existence of—much less the oppression suffered by—the millions of house-church Christians in China, though he was well versed in the human rights abuses suffered by Tibetan Buddhists, student democracy activists, and other Chinese groups. And when the Islamic judge in Kuwait raised the possibility of executing Christian convert Robert Hussein, the U.S. State Department issued a press advisory trivializing the fact that he was denied the right to see his children, giving unfounded assurances that he would not be killed.

The U.S. government has repeatedly failed to speak up for the religious rights of American citizens abroad. Take, for example, those Americans working for the U.S. government in Saudi Arabia who are restricted from holding Christian services on *American embassy grounds*, or those attending a 1995 United Nation's conference on Women in Beijing who were admonished by the U.S. State Department to leave their Bibles at home.

There is also the matter of asylum for religious refugees. In violation of its own laws, the U.S. has largely closed its doors to Christians fleeing for their lives from religious persecution. In the case of Christian refugees from Iran, the U.S. simply turns over the asylum determination to the Muslim police in Turkey, who summarily deport them back to their persecutors in Iran. Not one of some twenty clerics and religious leaders who fled Iran in the last two years received asylum in the United States.

And this from a country that was founded as a haven from religious persecution! Our government is ignoring our origin as a nation.

The Pilgrims, Quakers, Huguenots, Catholics, Jews, and legions of other religious minorities helped found and form this country as a safe haven from religious tyranny.

America's policy toward other nations should seek not only to meet the requirements of the oil trade and investors in new markets, but also to embody American values. Religious freedom is the bedrock value on which this country was founded. Religious liberty is not a privilege to be endowed by men, no matter how politically powerful they might be. It is a God-given human right—one that is recognized in the first clause of the First Amendment of the Constitution and in every major international agreement on civil and political rights.

America is a great power and wields tremendous influence. If the American president were to speak out on behalf of persecuted Christians and other religious minorities and exert pressure on their oppressors, it would bring dramatic results. Soviet refusniks Anatoly Shcharansky and Joseph Begun are alive today because the U.S. took up the campaign for Soviet Jewry. "How ironic and unacceptable," Hudson Institute scholar Michael Horowitz told Congress recently, "[that] the cause of Soviet Jewry was sustained and taken up as a *cause celebre* throughout America precisely because American Christians were so committed to its success, and now the Christian community is silent about the more pervasive persecution of its own people."[4]

Western Christians must take the lead in breaking the silence. If they don't speak out, no one will. Christians need to raise their voices to end the U.S. government's appalling neglect of the issue of Christian persecution abroad. As citizens in a democracy, "the American Christian community has right and reason to be heard," *Washington Post* deputy editor Stephen Rosenfeld recently wrote.[5] Richard John Neuhaus, a Catholic priest and president of Religion and Public Life, reasons: "Christians in this country need make no apology for insisting that their government demonstrate its concern for the persecution of fellow Christians. In fact, popular support for foreign policy in a democracy depends upon the responsiveness of the government to the concerns of the citizens."[6]

Once American Christians become informed and active in lending support to their oppressed brothers and sisters, and once their formidable political pressure is felt at home, there can be little doubt that the American public-at-large will respond with generous concern as it has in the past to other compelling instances of human rights victims, whether they be Soviet Jews, Romanian orphans, or Tibetan Buddhists.

For a variety of reasons, Christian churches have averted their eyes from religious persecution abroad since the end of the cold war. In some cases churches have lacked the information. In other cases they fear jeopardizing the access of their mission ministries in the oppressor country. Some have argued that the blood of martyrs waters the seeds of faith. Indeed, the witness of Christian martyrs has strengthened the Church from its beginnings. However, we must remember that in some cases, such as in many parts of the Muslim world, Christian communities are rapidly vanishing under relentless persecution.

Some Christians believe that it is the fate of Christians to be persecuted, using this as an excuse to do nothing. Ravi Zacharias strongly disagrees and argues that Christians are biblically mandated to intervene. "Reaching out with love is part of the Gospel's imperative," he writes. Dr. Zacharias reminds us that Jesus left the ninety-nine to go looking for the one. And the apostle Paul encouraged the Church of his time to take responsibility for the well-being of their fellow believers, saying, "Therefore, as we have opportunity, let us do good to all people, especially to those who belong to the family of believers" (Gal. 6:10). (Numerous other biblical passages instructing Christians to lend a helping hand to their fellow believers who are persecuted are in appendix D.)

The silence of the Western church may be coming to an end. A powerful new movement to defend persecuted Christians abroad has begun to coalesce among Western Christians. In January 1996, Freedom House convened a conference of some of the most influential religious leaders in the West to discuss ongoing human rights atrocities against Christians and strategies for ending the persecution. After that conference, commitments to speak out against the reigns of terror many Christians face were made by leaders of an impressive roster of large Christian churches and organizations, including the Southern Baptist Convention, the National Association of Evangelicals and many of its member denominations, Prison Fellowship Ministries, Ravi Zacharias International Ministries, the World Evangelical Fellowship, Coral Ridge Ministries, Focus on the Family, the Family Research Council, Campus Crusade for Christ, the Assemblies of God, the Lutheran Church-Missouri Synod, Open Doors, the Christian & Missionary Alliance, and the Institute on Religion and Democracy.

These religious leaders and activists organized an "International Day of Prayer for the Persecuted Church" that was observed in thousands of evangelical churches across the country on September 29, 1996. Some seventy thousand pastors received briefing materials about the issue, introducing many thousands of their congregants to the current persecution of Christians and encouraging them to remember their beleaguered brethren in prayer. In anticipation of this grassroots effort, both houses of the United States Congress unanimously adopted resolutions that "condemn the egregious human rights abuses and denials of religious liberty to Christians around the world" and "strongly recommend that the President expand and invigorate the United States' international advocacy on behalf of persecuted Christians and initiate a thorough examination" of relevant foreign policy.[7]

In January 1996, the National Association of Evangelicals (NAE) issued an unprecedented and forceful *Statement of Conscience and Call to Action* in which it pledged to end "our own silence in the face of the suffering of all those persecuted for their religious faith . . . [and] to do what is within our power to the end that the government of the United States will take appropriate action to combat the intolerable religious persecution now victimizing fellow believers and those of other faiths."[8] The NAE *Statement of Conscience* lists simple policy recommendations for the U.S. government to ensure that persecuted Christians and other religious minorities are not betrayed by American foreign policy.

The NAE *Statement of Conscience* has since been endorsed or commended by the Southern Baptist Convention, the Episcopal

Church, the Presbyterian Church, U.S.A., and the United Methodist Church.

The NAE *Statement of Conscience* is extraordinary because it addresses the need for systematic reform in U.S. foreign policy. Too many times, dealing with Christian persecution on a case-by-case basis becomes an exercise in futility. As the oppressive regime releases one well-known prisoner under international pressure, it imprisons twenty more whose names and cases are not known. Countries around the world must be given the message that it is the firm and consistent policy of the U.S. to grant zero tolerance to the persecutors of Christians and other religious minorities.

Pope John Paul II has always been a stalwart defender of religious freedom. During the Second Vatican Council, he was the chief drafter of the Catholic Church's "Declaration on Religious Liberty" and has since made it a central theme of his papacy. In his January 1996 address to the Diplomatic Corps, Pope John Paul II sounded an opening call against the persecution of Christians by Islamist and communist regimes in the name of "the most fundamental freedom —that of practicing one's faith openly, which for human beings is their reason for living."[9]

The interest expressed by these church leaders and ordinary Christians brings great hope for the fate of Christians now victimized for their faith by authoritarian regimes and in communal violence abroad. To be effective, however, this new campaign needs the *sustained* support of the American Christian community. All Christians share the obligation of intervening to help the suffering Church abroad. In the words of Prison Fellowship Ministries founder Chuck Colson, who addressed the Freedom House conference in January 1996, "The job of courageous leaders of the faith is to sear the consciences of the people."[10] They should remember the persecuted Christians in their prayers just as when Peter and Paul were imprisoned the whole Church gathered to pray for the release of the two disciples.

The American Christian community also needs to take political action and use its significant political leverage to press for actual reform in U.S. foreign policy. The widely-endorsed NAE *Statement of Conscience* states: "We know that the United States government has within its power and discretion the capacity to adopt policies that would be dramatically effective in curbing such reigns of terror and protecting the rights of all religious dissidents."[11]

Specific, achievable reforms that American citizens can press for are outlined in the NAE *Statement of Conscience*. Those with priority are:

- Publicly condemning Christian persecution and showing greater concern for persecuted Christians by the president and all appropriate branches of his administration;

- Improving reporting by the State Department Human Rights Bureau to ensure that its annual reports and other publications accurately reflect the situation facing Christians, eliminating from the annual reporting any "option of silence" regarding persecution;

- Appointing a special presidential advisor for religious liberty;

- Reforming the ways in which the Immigration and Naturalization Service treats the petitions of escapees from anti-Christian persecution; and,

- Terminating non-humanitarian foreign assistance to governments of countries that fail to take vigorous action to end anti-Christian or other religious persecution.

Campaigning to end anti-Christian persecution will help protect other persecuted religious groups and minorities as well. Buddhists in Tibet and Vietnam, Baha'is in Iran, Ahmadis in Pakistan, and animists in Sudan suffer persecution and death under the same practices and policies that oppress Christians in those countries. Moderate Muslims throughout northern Africa and the Middle East are now struggling against radical Islamists who seek to convert a historically tolerant Islam into an intolerant, anti-intellectual, anti-democratic faith. For all of these groups, Christian concern for religious freedom throughout the world offers the greatest prospect for freedom.

In Hebrews the Bible exhorts us to "Remember those in prison as if you were their fellow prisoners, and those who are mistreated as if you yourselves were suffering" (13:3). In the Book of Proverbs we are told, "Do not withhold good from those who deserve it, when it is in your power to act" (3:27). First Corinthians states about the Church, "If one part [of the body] suffers, every part suffers with it" (12:26), and Galatians directs us to "bear one another's burdens" (6:2). American Christians must begin to do all within their power to alleviate the suffering of those fellow Christians persecuted throughout the world for their religious beliefs.

In short, Christians have a special reason to provide leadership in this issue—leadership through prayer and through action. *In the Lion's Den* is designed to help give the American Christian community the facts and guidance for this endeavor.

> Nina Shea, Director
> Puebla Program on Religious Freedom
> Freedom House*
> October 29, 1996

---

*Freedom House was founded on a nonpartisan basis in 1941 by Eleanor Roosevelt and Wendell Willkie to rally Americans against isolationism in response to the dark age of totalitarianism—Nazism and Communism—that had fallen over Europe. It continues to promote an engaged U.S. foreign policy through a diverse range of programs that monitor human rights and elections; sponsor public education campaigns; offer training and technical assistance to promote democratic governance and free market reforms; and support the rule of law, religious freedom, a free media, and effective local governance. Freedom House publishes an annual survey of *Freedom in the World*, the most authoritative rating of the status of political rights and civil liberties in more than two hundred countries and territories around the world.

The Puebla Program on Religious Freedom was established within Freedom House in October 1995. The Puebla Program (formerly the Puebla Institute) has advocated the rights of persecuted Christians and other religious minorities throughout the world for ten years. Through on-site fact-finding investigations and other research, the Puebla Program documents instances of religious repression. It presents its findings and analysis before the U.S. Congress and in the media and other public forums. In January 1996, Freedom House's Puebla Program sponsored a consultation on the global persecution of Christians with more than one hundred leaders of key Christian organizations and churches.

CHAPTER 1

Prolonged Silence of American Christian Churches

WHILE CHRISTIANS IN MANY PARTS of the world increasingly face harassment, arrest, interrogation, imprisonment, or even death because of their religious beliefs, their co-religionists in the West have been strangely silent. A few Christian organizations have labored on religious liberty issues, trying to raise public awareness and advocate particular cases, but the majority of churches and Christian groups have stayed far from the fray.

There are numerous reasons for the lack of American Christian involvement in the issue, some stemming from differences in political ideology and others from practical or even theologically-based perceptions. Michael Novak, holder of the George Frederick Jewett Chair in Religion and Public Policy at the American Enterprise Institute in Washington, D.C., and winner of the Templeton Prize for Progress in Religion, observes

> The Christian church has a tradition of passivity and long-suffering. The awakening occurred in domestic matters in the emergence of a vocal conservative activist wing of Christians. This Christian wing is one of the great events of the last twenty years, but it has taken a little longer for it to acquire an international dimension. A certain self-confidence is required. On the other hand, the Christian left was so busy issuing warnings against conservatives and against anti-communism that there was a tendency to constantly be apologizing for or minimizing persecution of the faith under left-wing dictatorships (including Arab socialism).[1]

As a result, many Western Christians are simply unaware of the extent to which their fellow believers continue to suffer today. "When the Iron Curtain fell, people thought, 'Oh good, the Christians are free now.' But persecution is still very real," says Christopher Catherwood, visiting scholar at Cambridge University's Center of International Studies.[2]

There are a few good sources of information about ongoing persecution. Freedom House's Puebla Program on Religious Freedom and several other human rights and religious liberty organizations do monitor the situation. However, there has been a serious lack of significant media coverage about religious persecution in both the mainstream and religious press.

Another difficulty is that oppressed Christians often do not tell their own stories. For them, persecution is just "a fact of life when you are a Christian," says David Stravers, executive vice-president of the Bible League, an evangelistic agency that supports Chinese churches.[3] Also, many Christians seek to avoid bringing attention to their own history of persecution due to fear of retribution.

There are times, however, when Western Christian groups are aware of persecution but make the intentional decision not to get involved because of practical considerations about retaining access to oppressive countries. This has been especially true regarding many missionary agencies and relief and development organizations. "In several circumstances, it is clear that Christian organizations either maintain silence about persecution or indeed gloss over it in order to maintain their own work in a particular country or achieve access," says Paul Marshall, senior fellow at the Institute for Christian Studies in Toronto.[4] "If your work in China depends on getting government permission to be there, you are reluctant to go around publicizing that the government is mistreating its citizens," notes Stravers, whose own organization often works outside government channels.[5]

Marshall, author of *Their Blood Cries Out,* a book on the persecution of Christians, also faults the liberal churches as having been unwilling to speak out on Christian persecution because of their "reluctance to criticize left-wing regimes, their focus on the faults of the U.S., their desire to maintain 'good relations' with 'dialogue partners,' and their general suspicion of evangelicals and evangelicalism, which see the most persecution."[6]

According to Marshall, many modern American Christians are too preoccupied with their own quest for inner peace to be concerned about persecution. "Many evangelicals in particular seem to be so obsessed with their own well-being that they cannot get their noses out of their own navels to pay attention to the plight of their brothers and sisters around the world," says Marshall.[7]

He notes other theological issues may be at work as well. Some fundamentalists and charismatics, in particular, may be reluctant to stop persecution because they see it as part of a fulfillment of end-times prophecy.

Other Christians across the theological spectrum may take a fatalistic or even romantic view of martyrs and persecuted Christians. In the Bible Jesus Christ warned that His followers would suffer persecution. Although history has shown that some of the largest spurts of church growth emerged from periods of persecution, in some places like the Middle East, persecution has led to a vastly diminished Christian presence. In Iraq the number of Christians has decreased from 35 percent to 5 percent of the overall population; in Iran, from 15 percent to 2 percent; in Syria, from 40 percent to 10 percent; and in Turkey, from 32 percent to 0.2 percent since the early part of the twentieth century.

Yet many church leaders disagree with the premise that Christians should not seek to eliminate suffering and persecution simply because the Bible predicts that they will occur. Reg Reimer, director of World Evangelical Fellowship's Department of Church and Society and a longtime president of World Relief Canada, points to biblical stories that describe how the Apostle Paul responded to religious persecution: "Sometimes he fled; sometimes he suffered and endured; but sometimes he resisted, such as when he used his Roman citizenship to appeal the charges against him. He used every legal means that he had in order not to suffer."[8]

Catholic priest Richard John Neuhaus, president of Religion and Public Life, observes: "We all bear a great responsibility for changing the situation. Again and again, Pope John Paul II has reminded us that all human rights have their source and shield in religious freedom. That message needs to be much more effectively communicated than it has been to date." [9]

"The Bible also says that the poor will always be with us, but at the same time it urges Christians to give food to the hungry and clothes to the naked," points out Diane Knippers, president of the Institute on Religion and Democracy. "We must take the same compassionate approach to those suffering from religious persecution. Persecution is evil. It is a sin on the part of the persecutors which should be denounced." [10]

CHAPTER 2

Western Failure

WHILE THE CHURCH HAS BEEN GENERALLY silent on the issue of Christian persecution, Western society at large has done no better.

Religious liberty is enshrined in the United States Constitution. The United States itself is a nation founded by religious refugees seeking the right to practice their faith without persecution. Even on the international level, the right to religious liberty is clearly guaranteed by international human rights covenants and United Nations declarations.

Yet on a consistent basis, Western journalists, scholars, diplomats, international analysts, and politicians either ignore incidents of Christian persecution or downplay their significance.

Much of the news media are either unaware of stories of Christian persecution or unwilling to see "news value" in the stories. Few scholars discuss the issue in academic publications or university settings. Tensions between Christians and Muslims are seen as "ethnic" or "political" conflicts rather than religious ones. The few who do recognize the religious dimensions of political trends rarely address the impact on religious liberty.

Western politicians seldom, if ever, make any situations of religious persecution—much less the persecution of Christians—a major foreign policy concern. Even secular human rights organizations, which have occasionally launched successful campaigns on behalf of Christian prisoners of conscience, all too often give lower priority to cases of persecution against Christians than to other human rights violations.

"An increasingly secularized West and its leadership elite tend to be indifferent and often uncomprehending of a spiritual worldview which endures persecution and death for the sake of belief," says Richard Land, president of the Southern Baptist Convention

Christian Life Commission. "Too often people in the West, peering through the selective prism of Christian history in the West, reflexively think of Christians as persecutors, rather than the persecuted."[1]

Paul Marshall calls the phenomenon a "Western, secular myopia" that leads to a "truncated view of the world."[2] Such an outlook, he and others argue, results not only in the marginalization of Christian persecution, but also in a crucial lack of information needed to accurately understand world events.

Richard John Neuhaus agrees:

> As in domestic policy, so also in foreign policy, the U.S. government has tended to be religiously tone-deaf. This is not—or not usually—the result of hostility to religion. It is, rather, a habit of mind that has been dominant since the eighteenth-century Enlightenment, in which there is a sharp dichotomy—frequently a divorce—between the "religious" and the "secular." In this view, the "religion factor" is removed from the "real world" of politics among nations. As a result, religious persecution tends to be viewed as a subset of "human rights" concerns and, as we know, human rights does not have a secure place in the hierarchy of considerations taken seriously by the foreign policy establishment.[3]

Indeed, a few analysts have suggested that the growing persecution of Christians is an outcome of a close relationship between Christianity and the growth of democracy in parts of Eastern Europe, Latin America, and Asia. In a widely discussed 1993 article in *Foreign Affairs* journal, political scientist Samuel Huntington asserted that clashing "civilizations" categorized by religion would be the basis of much coming world conflict.[4] Ironically, while religious freedom issues tend to be overlooked by policy makers in the West, religion is playing an increasingly greater role in world events.

Some scholars believe evangelical Protestants and Catholics are being persecuted by those who seek to "hold back" the twenty-first century. "Christians are the greatest forces for modernity in its best sense throughout the world," says Michael Horowitz, senior fellow at the Hudson Institute think tank in Washington, D.C. "Inherent in the Christian commitment is the notion of individual dignity and worth, the notion that no state power can ultimately threaten or bribe them away from more abiding convictions."[5]

Horowitz argues that Christians—evangelical Protestants in particular—have become the "perfect scapegoats" for threatened totalitarian regimes. At the same time, he says, "Western elites" and fellow Christians in the West have been mostly "indifferent, embarrassed and uncertain" about the situation. "What could be a more perfect prescription for persecution?" he asks.[6]

Land agrees: "Christians are threats to the anti-democratic forces which oppose modernity, and if the Western secular elites do not understand this—make no mistake—the Chinese, Vietnamese and Cuban commissars and the Islamic ayatollahs do."[7]

Unfortunately, American foreign policy has suffered greatly from this secularized thinking. And nowhere has this been more evident than in the realm of religious liberty. As Michael Novak observes: "There has been a tradition in the State Department of turning a blind eye to religion and taking an excessively secular approach to world affairs."[8]

George Weigel, senior fellow of the Washington-based Ethics and Public Policy Center, states, "In the 1980s American foreign policy was a vigorous force in defense of the church in communist societies. Why those same criteria are not applied in countries today when Christians are under great pressure is a puzzle. Is there secular myopia? An unwillingness to face the realities of life in certain Islamic societies? Is there a general nervousness with asserting the moral truth of the universality of human rights? I suspect elements of all three are involved."[9]

America used to stand firmly for human rights values, but since the end of the cold war, this sense of purpose is being lost. Today, U.S. politicians barely mention human rights at all. American policy appears to be increasingly dominated by trade and environmentalism, the new foreign policy fashions. The United States no longer sends the message that it cares deeply about religious freedom.

For example, when President Clinton met with his Chinese counterpart in October 1995 at the United Nations in New York, he proclaimed that the greatest threat China now poses to the world is pollution. U.S. officials also vigorously spoke out against Chinese piracy of American computer software and compact discs. Yet no official statements were made expressing concern that Chinese authorities are now waging the greatest crackdown against Protestant house-church members and Roman Catholics since the late 1970s.

In general, architects of American foreign policy—including those at the highest levels—show a shocking ignorance about the plight of persecuted Christians. Consider the case of James Sasser, the new U.S. ambassador to China. Sasser spent nine months being briefed by the State Department for his new post. Yet during a January 1996 meeting with religious liberty advocates on the eve of his departure for Beijing, Sasser displayed a breathtaking gap in his education. When the religious liberty activists expressed their concerns about growing repression against the tens of millions of Chinese Christians who attend underground house churches, Sasser asked, "What's a house church?"[10]

The State Department's annual comprehensive human rights reports also fail to adequately reflect understanding of religious persecution. While the 1996 report was generally an accurate assessment of human rights practices worldwide, the sections on "Freedom of Religion" were the weakest areas of coverage.[11] In many cases, the report did not adequately distinguish among various Christian denominations, but instead, generalized the experience of the dominant religious group that usually has the most freedom. In several important instances the report also failed to address the role of society in persecuting religious minorities while a passive government did nothing to stop the terror.

Weaknesses in the "Freedom of Religion" section of the State Department report are especially important because of their practical application to other parts of U.S. policy, such as in the area of granting political asylum to refugees fleeing persecution. In recent years, immigration judges around the country relied on the State

Department's report to deny political asylum to numerous Christians fleeing persecution.

Among those who recently spent long periods in immigration detention or were denied asylum outright are a Sudanese Christian who could not explain the theological doctrine of transubstantiation to the satisfaction of the immigration judge; a Pakistani Christian who was acquitted of the capital crime of blasphemy but feared mob retribution; more than twenty Iranian clergy and religious leaders who fled the country after three of their colleagues were murdered; and numerous Chinese Christians fleeing forced abortions and sterilizations.

Michael Horowitz, who has attempted to help several Ethiopian evangelicals come to the United States, says: "Immigration lawyers tell me that it's easier to pass a camel through a needle's eye than to get an asylum claim satisfied for a Christian who has escaped persecution."[12]

Several groups, including the U.S.-based Iranian Christians International, have raised particular concerns about how U.S. officials handle the processing of Iranian Christian refugees coming to Turkey. Abe Ghaffari, executive director of Iranian Christians International, attested before Congress on February 15, 1996:

> In July 1994, the U.S. Immigration and Naturalization Service adopted a policy requiring that all refugee applicants be recognized as refugees by the United Nations High Commissioner for Refugees before being interviewed by the U.S. Immigration and Naturalization Service. Prior to that time, applicants were allowed to apply directly to the U.S. Consulate. At the same time, the UN High Commissioner for Refugees turned over all of its refugee processing and decision-making authority to the Turkish government. . . . The resulting attitude and behavior of the Turkish police toward the Muslim converts or apostates is often hostile and abusive. The net effect of the above changes in procedure is that not a single Iranian Christian has immigrated to the U.S. from Turkey in the last eighteen months.[13]

The adversarial attitude of U.S. INS officials and inconsistent refugee processing has led to refugees finding themselves between a rock and a hard place. They cannot go back to Iran, yet the governments of the countries in which they have found temporary residence threaten them with deportation and, in some cases, deport them back to Iran. Many of the refugees are also financially destitute and cannot survive unnecessarily drawn-out appeals.[14]

During a November 1995 meeting with human rights activists, John Shattuck, assistant secretary for Democracy, Human Rights, and Labor, asserted that religious liberty remains "a major topic" in the Clinton human rights agenda. "We feel strongly about issues of religious liberty," he said.[15]

However, there has been little action to back up such words. In early 1996, the administration considered the appointment of an advisor to specialize in religious liberty issues, but by mid-1996, disagreements about the nature of the position had blocked such an appointment. By fall 1996, the administration instead turned to the idea of convening an advisory committee whose members would have diverse religious affiliations and interests and who would report to the secretary of state, not the president.

The National Association of Evangelicals invited President Clinton to speak at the association's annual convention in March 1996 in Minneapolis on the topic of religious liberty. At a meeting with evangelicals in the Oval Office, President Clinton initially appeared favorable about the invitation. However, he did not attend the meeting; Presidential aides said there was not enough money in the budget for the airfare to Minnesota.

With the exception of isolated individuals such as National Security Council advisor Richard Schifter—who used his position as the U.S. Ambassador to the United Nations Human Rights Commission in 1993 to denounce religious persecution against Christians and others around the globe and was the driving force behind the creation of a religious liberty advisory position in 1996—the U.S. government has overall been remiss in taking action or asserting positions in specific country situations to defend against anti-Christian persecution.

Congress has also done little on the issue of persecution of Christians. Specific attention to the issue has been devoted by a small and surprisingly bipartisan coalition of representatives and senators including Rep. Frank Wolf (R-VA), Rep. Chris Smith (R-NJ), Rep. Tony Hall (D-OH), Rep. Tom Lantos (D-CA), Rep. John Porter (R-IL), Sen. Richard Lugar (R-IL), Sen. Sam Nunn (D-GA) and Sen. Jesse Helms (R-NC). But there has been little overall congressional action or legislation that is binding on U.S. policy. During the Soviet era a Democratic Congress passed the Jackson-Vanik bill linking economic and trade relations to the treatment of Soviet Jews and other minorities. However, since the collapse of the Soviet Union, neither a Democratic nor a Republican Congress has been able to pass similar bipartisan bills linking trade benefits to human rights in China. Many members of Congress have expressed concern that such legislation would hurt U.S. business interests abroad.

Attention to the persecution of Christians has also been lacking at the international policy level. At the highly touted United Nations World Conference on Women held in August 1995 in Beijing, the draft entitled "Platform for Action"—written by the leaders of 189 nations—contained more than 120 pages of affirmations of women's rights, from environmental rights to economic rights. But there was not a single mention of the right to religious freedom in the entire document. Only after last-minute aggressive lobbying by a small group of nongovernmental participants led by the Institute on Religion and Democracy did the United Nations conference finally agree to include language reiterating women's universal right to religious freedom.

The issue of Christian persecution was also given short shrift at the 1996 United Nations Human Rights Commission meeting in Geneva. During much of the human rights discussion, neither the United States nor other Western delegations spoke out forcefully and explicitly about Christian persecution. For example, according to Wilfred Wong of the British-based human rights group Jubilee

Campaign, the European Union gave a nineteen-page statement expressing its concern about the most pervasive human rights violations in the world. Tibetan Buddhists and Baha'is in Iran were specifically singled out, but there were no specific references to the persecution of Christians.

"That was very, very disappointing, considering that the fifteen European Union states are basically from a Christian background," Wong says. "If the countries of a Christian background have so little interest in specifically referring to the persecution of Christians, then who will?"[16]

Wong believes governments are not fully to blame for these failures to speak up forcefully on behalf of persecuted Christians. He states, "If Christians themselves don't have a deep awareness or concern on these issues, then it's hardly surprising when their governments fail to reflect such an awareness and concern."[17]

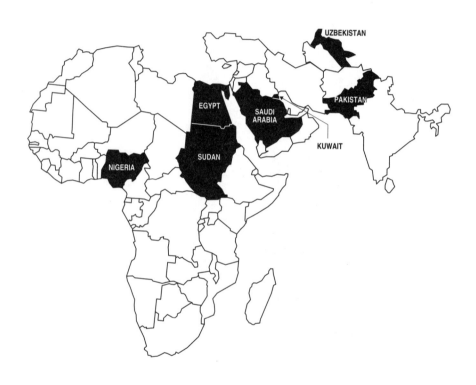

CHAPTER 3

Perdecution in Islamic Countries

LATE IN MAY 1996, THE MUTILATED corpses of seven French Trappist monks were discovered in Algeria. The monks had been kidnapped two months earlier by members of the Armed Islamic Group, a radical Islamist organization fighting for control of the North African nation of Algeria. The French government had refused to negotiate for the release of the hostages. After two months these radicals slit the throats of the seven monks. Moderate Muslims condemned the murders. A month later, two Muslim rebels shot and wounded a leading moderate Algerian Muslim cleric while he was praying in a mosque.

Both incidents are part of the ongoing civil strife in Algeria as militant Muslim extremists wage a violent battle to take political control of the nation. The violence began with a vengeance in 1992 after government authorities canceled an election that the militant Islamists seemed poised to win.

A BATTLE FOR THE SOUL OF ISLAM

Many scholars believe what is taking place in Algeria typifies a trend through the Islamic world where an increasingly radical and militant form of Islam seeks political dominance. As this movement spreads across Africa and Asia, Christians and moderate Muslims are seen as obstacles or even active opponents. David F. Forte, professor of law at Cleveland State University, states that a battle for the very soul of Islam is under-way. Some of the worst persecution faced by Christians today is happening on the front lines of these battle zones. Silence from the West in the face of religious suppression not only betrays the persecuted Christians, but it also leaves beleaguered and vulnerable the majority of Muslim communities.

27

The following discussion on pages 28–30 was adapted from testimony delivered by Professor Forte before the House of Representatives Subcommittee on International Operations and Human Rights on February 15, 1996:

· · · ·

THE KHARIJITE HERESY

During the first century of Islam, barely four decades after the death of Mohammed, a terrible rebellion broke out in the new Islamic Empire. On one side was the wing that would eventually become the majority Sunni branch of Islam. On the other was the wing that would constitute the Shiite branch of Islam. But those who rebelled against both wings were the Kharijites, whose battles and theology were terrible indeed.

The Kharijites believed that any Muslim who committed a sin was an apostate, an unbeliever who could never reenter the fold of Islam and who must be killed. Any leader who did not follow the strict practice of Islam must be overthrown. The Kharijites fought brutally to become the one and only version of Islam. They were finally suppressed, but not until more than one hundred years later.

Today, a modern version of Kharijite heresy stalks Islam. It has gained the reins of power in Iran and Sudan. It threatens Algeria, Bangladesh, Egypt, even Saudi Arabia. It cows a timid government in Pakistan to accede to its program. It persecutes minorities, particularly Christians. But its real objective is to steal the soul of Islam, to change that religion's tradition of art, culture, learning, and toleration into its own image of rigid and tyrannical power.

THE SHARI'A

These extremists claim the support of the *Shari'a*—the sacred law of Islam—and especially seek to enforce its criminal provisions against adultery, alcohol, theft, and apostasy. But little do these modern-day radicals realize that the criminal portions of the *Shari'a*—the most notorious being stoning for adultery, amputation for theft, and death for apostasy—are the least developed parts of the *Shari'a*.

These portions are the least developed because the Islamic state always kept nearly all criminal jurisdiction to itself. There was never a time in the history of Islam when the portions of the *Shari'a* dealing with criminal offenses were enforced with the literalness their adherents now claim for it.

Today, however, the ancient rules of the *Shari'a*—hardly observed even in the days when they were formulated—are used in a program more akin to political tyranny than to religion.

In Pakistan, for example, the law against blasphemy is being used by some to terrorize Christians, who are among the poorest and most socially rejected of Pakistan's peoples. The law against blasphemy has had two effects: First, it directly attacks religious minorities who are supposedly guaranteed their rights by Pakistan's constitution and the international law of Human Rights. Secondly, the law loosens and legitimizes private acts of terror against Christians by unfettered Muslims who believe—and who have been told by radical Islamic religious leaders—that they have a right to attack blasphemers and apostates directly with legal impunity.

THE SILENT UNITED STATES

The United States has been an ineffective friend (if a friend at all) to persecuted Christians and other religious minorities under the thumb of Islamic radicals. By not using our substantial influence to inform our allies that the radicals' laws and actions are against international law and that they offend the basic sense of decency of the American people, we send the following messages:

- We don't believe in protecting those religious adherents of the West, and we must be the materialist bankrupt culture the Islamic radicals claim we are.

- Radical Islam is a legitimate force in the world, and it is all right with us if—for reasons of state—Islamic governments give in to the radicals' tyrannical agenda.

- We treat our Islamic friends with patronizing indifference. After all, we, in effect, say that this is not a human rights problem but a Muslim problem.

Our inactivity helps create regimes and forces whose ultimate aim is to destroy the West as well as the tradition of Islam. Imagine if we took a neutral or disinterested view of the radicals who murdered Israeli Prime Minister Yitzhak Rabin. Yet this is not the case. In fact, we accept and champion the view of the majority of Jews that those who commit acts of violence *supposedly* in the name of Jewish law are not part of genuine Judaism at all.

We have the same moral obligation—and indeed the same enlightened self-interest—to treat the religion of Islam in a similar fashion. We should show our support and respect for the vast majority of Muslims who reject those who practice violence as being un-Islamic.

We should see these movements for what they are. They are not religious. Let us never legitimize them with that name and insult hundreds of millions of Muslims. These movements are rather a new form of political tyranny. You can tell a person by his fruits, and the fruits of political tyranny always have been a frontal attack on religious minorities. It is happening today, and the longer it is allowed to happen, the worse it will be for both millions of Christians and millions of Muslims.

• • • •

COUNTRY PROFILES

SUDAN

In 1992, a nine-year-old Christian boy from the Sudanese Dinka tribe was sent to the market by his mother to buy tomatoes. Sudan's ongoing civil war had forced the boy's family from their home, and they  were living in a displaced persons' camp in Omdurman. While on his errand, the boy was stopped by Muslim police. He showed them the money his mother had given him and tried to explain what he was doing, but no one would listen. "I was put into a police truck with many other black boys and taken away," he says.[1]

The boys spent seven days in Khartoum, the capital, where they were beaten repeatedly. Then they were taken to Fau, a children's "cultural cleansing" camp. There the beatings continued, and the kidnapped boys were forcibly converted to Islam.

"We were awakened at 4:00 in the morning and forced to pray out loud, memorizing Koranic verses by heart," the Dinka boy said. "All day we alternated between Islamic training and military marching. If one made a mistake, he was beaten, and the rest were punished with him."[2]

This boy eventually escaped from the camp and made his way back to his mother. He recounted his story to Freedom House investigator Kevin Vigilante, who traveled to northern Sudan in 1995. But thousands of other Sudanese children are not so fortunate. Vigilante and the Freedom House fact-finding team documented widespread government-sponsored abductions of children, part of a campaign of "cultural cleansing" targeted at African Christians and animists.

Forced to give up their religion, these children are prepared for use as cannon fodder in Sudan's lengthy civil war. The children, many with families, are snatched by government agents from public places in the capital and other northern cities. They are summarily detained in high-security, closed camps for children where they are given new Arabic names, indoctrinated in Islam, and forced to undergo military-style training. Within the camps, disease is rampant and food scarce. The government refuses access to international relief and church groups that seek to provide assistance to these children.

Kidnapping is just one of the many grim fates awaiting Sudanese Christians who have been locked in civil war for more than a decade with the National Islamic Front government based in Khartoum. The war has pitted the predominantly Arab and Islamic north against the predominantly Christian and animist south. Islamic fundamentalists declared Sudan an Islamic state in 1983, and government attempts to apply *Shari'a* (Islamic law) to all citizens was one of the key factors leading to war.

The militant Islamic government's scorched-earth and forced-starvation tactics as it prosecutes its religious war in the southern, Christian part of the country have resulted in the deaths of more than 1.3 million people and the displacement of more than 3 million others, mostly Christians and non-Muslims.

To eradicate the Christian and non-Muslim population, the Sudanese government and its agents have bombed, burned and looted southern villages; enslaved women and children; kidnapped and forcibly converted Christians and other boys and sent them into battle; relocated entire villages into concentration camps called "peace villages"; and withheld food aid to starving Christian and animist communities until they converted to Islam.

Individual Christians, including clergy, have been assassinated, imprisoned, tortured, and flogged for their faith. There have been numerous reports of Christians being crucified in remote areas, but given the ongoing war and difficulty of access, no outside investigators have been able to independently confirm the reports.

The United Nations Human Rights Commission and numerous independent human rights investigators have all acknowledged that Christians and animists continue to be targets of a brutal government-sponsored campaign of "forced Islamization." For example, the

FIGURE 3–1
Young Christian boys in Sudan are frequently kidnapped and taken to "cultural cleansing camps" where they are forcibly converted to Islam. The displaced persons camp in southern Sudan where these children took refuge was bombed by Sudan's military shortly after this photo was taken (Note the beads with cross around the neck of the boy at left). *Credit: Charles J. Brown, Freedom House's Puebla Program on Religious Freedom*

FIGURE 3–2
In Sudan, the radical Islamic government condones the capture and sale of Christians and other non-Muslims at open-air slave markets. In this photo taken in early 1996, Christian Solidarity International worker John Eibner poses with two Christian boys, Bol (left)

and Deng Kuol (right), who had just been redeemed from enslavement and were waiting to be reunited with their families. *Credit: Christian Solidarity International*

UN Special Rapporteur on Sudan, Gaspar Biro, reported that in May 1995, soldiers in uniform summarily executed twelve men, women, and children at Lobonok for refusing to convert to Islam.[4]

In February 1996, Biro also reported "an alarming increase" in the number of cases of "slavery, servitude, slave trade, and forced labor" in Sudan.[5] With ghastly frequency villages in southern Sudan are raided. The men are systematically killed while their property is either confiscated or destroyed. The women and children are abducted and transferred north, sold into slavery as servants, housekeepers, and concubines.

Even as this book goes to press, Christian women and children are being bought and sold—some for as little as $15—in the thriving chattel slave market. Christian Solidarity International reports that more than twenty-five thousand children from the Nuba Mountain region alone have been abducted and sold into slavery.[6] Bishop Macram Max Gassis, the international spokesman for the Catholic Bishops' Conference of Sudan, has been actively raising money in Europe (where he is in exile) to buy back the children of the villages in El Obeid, his diocese.

In a 1994 report to the United Nations Commission on Human Rights, Biro cited the locations of camps where "people from northern Sudan or even from abroad" come to buy captured Christians and animists as slaves.[7] To prevent the captured Christians from escaping, they are branded or mutilated. A southern Christian boy told the Freedom House team that he was enslaved by an Arab master who cut the Achilles tendons of male slaves who did not convert to Islam. The boy converted to Islam to avoid this fate and later managed to escape. A young Christian girl interviewed by Freedom House displayed a large scar on her thigh—the mark of a brand she received while enslaved by a Muslim master in northern Sudan.[8]

FIGURE 3–3
Mother and child in a displaced persons camp in southern Sudan. Government soldiers have pressured Christians to convert to Islam or face starvation for themselves and their children. *Credit: Charles J. Brown, Freedom House's Puebla Program on Religious Freedom*

All the world was able to witness the sale of Christian slaves when the *Baltimore Sun*—with the help of Christian Solidarity International—proved beyond a doubt that chattel slavery remains an ongoing practice in Sudan despite the denials of the Islamic fundamentalist government and its supporters.[9] Starting on June 16, 1996, the *Sun* ran three front-page articles with powerful photographs detailing how two of its reporters went to Sudan and bought two slaves for five hundred dollars each, whom they immediately returned to their families.

FIGURE 3–4

Bishop Macram Max Gassis, the Catholic bishop of El Obeid Diocese in Sudan, though forced into exile by the government of Sudan, secretly returns to his homeland at great personal risk in order to buy freedom for children of all religious affiliations sold into slavery by Muslim forces. *Credit: Christian Solidarity International*

In Sudan, it is also a capital offense to convert to Christianity. In August 1995, five Nuban woman were sentenced to death for apostasy or abandoning Islam. In late 1995, ten people were arrested for converting to Christianity.

Sudanese law prohibits any proselytizing of Muslims. The regular activities of the Sudan Catholic Bishops' Conference, the Sudan Council of Churches, and the Coptic Church are often hindered by government officials. Christian missionary groups are required to apply for special licenses, and there are frequent delays or denials of work permits for religious workers. The government continues to deny permission to build churches; no new churches have been built in the North since the early 1970s. In October 1996, Khartoum announced strict new Islamic regulations to segregate males and females in public places and at social gatherings in the northern part of the country.

"The government of Sudan continues to try to transform by force the ethnically and religiously diverse country into an Arab, Islamic state against the wishes of the vast majority of its population, both North and South," says Baroness Caroline Cox, who works with Christian Solidarity International. "The devastating effects of this policy in the South and the Nuba Mountains are tantamount to genocide."[10]

PAKISTAN

Fifteen-year-old Salamat Masih has a price on his head. In the past two years the Pakistani Christian youth has been arrested on blasphemy charges, imprisoned, shot at, convicted, sentenced

to death, acquitted, and forced into hiding. He now lives in Germany, where he and his codefendant fled after their 1995 acquittal in a highly publicized blasphemy trial. Still, Masih watches his back: Muslim militants have offered as much as thirty thousand dollars to anyone who kills him.

Masih and two other Christians, Manzoor Masih and Rehmat Masih (no relation), were arrested in Pakistan in May 1993, accused of writing derogatory slogans about the prophet Mohammed on the wall of the village mosque. Under Pakistani law, the death penalty must be imposed on "whoever by words, either spoken or written . . . or by any imputation, innuendo, or insinuation, directly or indirectly, defiles the sacred name of the Holy Prophet [Mohammed]."[11]

The case was controversial from the start. There was no evidence of the alleged crime. The accuser, a Muslim cleric, claimed the words were so offensive that he immediately washed them off the mosque wall before anyone else could read them. He also refused to repeat the words in the courtroom. Salamat Masih, who was twelve years old at the time of his arrest, was only semi-literate.

The three defendants were eventually granted bail while their trial proceeded. In April 1994, armed gunmen attacked the three after a court hearing. Manzoor Masih was killed, and Salamat and Rehmat were both wounded. The surviving defendants were finally convicted of blasphemy in February 1995 and sent to death row. However, in an unprecedented speedy appeal that was undoubtedly due to international pressure, the Lahore High Court overturned the convictions just two weeks later. But outrage among Islamic extremists forced the two Masihs to flee Pakistan for their lives.

Pakistan is a predominantly Muslim country that has several religious minorities—including Christians, Hindus, and Ahmadis, who belong to an outlawed Islamic sect. According to many human rights advocates, the blasphemy laws have created a hostile atmosphere for these minorities. Extremist Muslims believe they have the right to carry out the death sentence extrajudicially, and several Christians accused of blasphemy have been murdered by angry mobs.

While Pakistan has had legislation against blasphemy since the British colonial era, military dictator Zia ul Haq enacted several changes in 1986 to impose the death penalty and make the laws specific to Islam.

According to the nongovernmental Human Rights Commission of Pakistan, more than five hundred blasphemy cases are currently pending in Pakistani courts—many involving Christians and Ahmadis. Amnesty International reports that, in all known cases to date, "the charges appear to have been arbitrarily brought, founded solely on the individuals' minority religious beliefs or on malicious accusations against individuals who advocate novel ideas from the Muslim majority community."[12]

One of the most prominent current blasphemy cases is that of Anwar Yaqoob Masih, who has remained in prison since 1993 when he was accused of uttering "blasphemous phrases against the prophet Mohammed."[13] Muslim extremists have vowed to kill Masih if the courts fail to convict him. (Note: Masih, which means "messiah," is a common surname for Christians in Pakistan.)

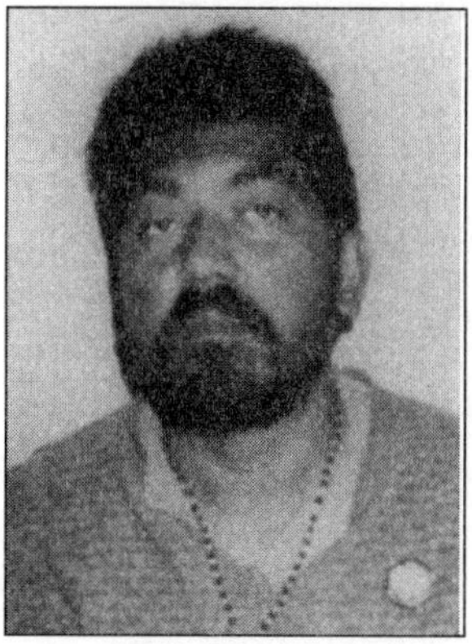

FIGURE 3–5

Anwar Yaqoob Masih is detained in Sammundri District Prison in Pakistan under accusations of "slighting the Prophet" because he is Christian. Married with three children, he is currently being kept with prisoners who are classified as criminally insane. This photo was taken in prison. *Credit: Open Doors*

Former Pakistan Prime Minister Benazir Bhutto made public promises to revise the blasphemy laws.[14] However, attempts by her government to introduce significant changes were sidelined by threats of a violent backlash by Islamist extremists. The government seemed weak in the face of pressure from extremist Islamic groups.

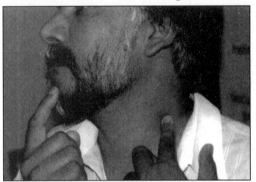

FIGURE 3–6
Pakistani Christian John Joseph was shot through the mouth and neck by Muslim extremists though he was found "not guilty" after being charged under Pakistan's blasphemy law, a capital offense that is frequently leveled against Christians. *Credit: Voice of the Martyrs*

Beyond the controversial blasphemy laws, Christians have been targeted by a general climate of violence and discrimination. Entire Christian communities have faced persecution by their neighbors and by local police who act with impunity. Numerous Christians have been forced from their villages by Muslim mobs. For example, the Muslim population of Khan Jajja and the surrounding localities were incited in May 1994 by the local Muslim cleric to drive the sixty Christian families of the region from the "land of the pure" and to demolish their church. The Christian men were beaten and the women were stripped naked in the rural tradition of revenge, while three girls were kidnapped and raped. These Christians' homes were razed and their possessions looted or destroyed. They fled to other villages in the district. Restitution for them is out of the question.[15]

On August 3, 1996, a Muslim lynch mob attempted to abduct a popular young Christian professor from the government college in Komalia after other professors belonging to the extremist group *Sipaha-e-Sohabah Pakistan* accused him of blasphemy. Professor Peter John was rescued from certain death by his Muslim neighbors and was able to go into hiding with the help of the Christian community. His experience with persecution has given other well-educated and successful Pakistani Christians reason to worry.

FIGURE 3–7
Munir Khokher was wounded by gunshot while trying to stop the destruction of a Christian cemetery by Muslim mobs in Pakistan. *Credit: Voice of the Martyrs*

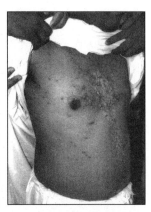

Christians are also victims in the growing number of deaths while in police custody. On August 4, 1995, Pakistani Christian Javid Masih, thirty-two, was tortured to death during a police interrogation. Witnesses said police used electric shock and other devices to compel Masih to confess to a robbery that he denied committing. The government filed charges against the three Muslim police officers involved, but no arrests have been made.

"Active persecution of minority religions is afoot, and governmental policy has let loose private acts of vengeance against Ahmadis, Christians, Hindus, pagans, and minority Muslim sects," says David Forte, professor of law at Cleveland State University. "The radicals who are the engine of these policies seek a version of Islam dramatically at odds with the vision of Pakistan's founders."[16]

FIGURE 3–8
Getaneh M. Getaneh, an evangelical Christian, has been arrested and imprisoned four times, interrogated and repeatedly tortured in Ethiopia because of his evangelistic activities, which were often targeted at Muslims. He describes being suspended from the ceiling by his feet for hours while prison guards poured hot oil on the soles of his feet. In 1985, he decided to flee to Djibouti. After the fall of Ethiopia's communist regime, Getaneh returned to his homeland in May 1994, having been assured by officials at the Ethiopian Embassy in Djibouti that things had changed. However, he was arrested and detained at the airport in Addis Ababa soon after his flight landed. After friends helped secure his release, he again fled to the United States seeking asylum. But his plight is by no means resolved. Officials at the U.S. Immigration and Naturalization Service denied his petition for asylum on the basis of religious persecution. The INS has issued a deportation order against Getaneh, determining that there is "no evidence" to substantiate his claim that he would be persecuted if he returned to Ethiopia. He is appealing. *Credit: Puebla Program on Religious Freedom, Freedom House*

Saudi Arabia

In the Kingdom of Saudi Arabia no public expression of Christianity is permitted. It is even illegal to wear a cross necklace, read a Bible, or utter a Christian prayer in the privacy of your own home.

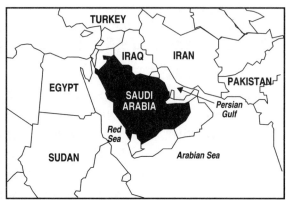

Five times a day, one billion Muslims around the world turn toward the Saudi city of Mecca to pray. But in its role as the keeper of global Islam, the Saudi Arabian government does not tolerate any practice of non-Muslim religions—either by its own citizens or by foreigners. All public and private Christian worship is completely banned, and all churches, Christian artifacts, and non-Muslim literature—including the Bible—are forbidden.

Freedom of religion simply does not exist in Saudi Arabia.

Under the law, conversion to Christianity by Saudi citizens is a criminal offense punishable by death. Christian foreign workers have been beaten and arrested for attempting to conduct clandestine worship services (some 4.6 million expatriates live and work in the kingdom—a full quarter of the Saudi population).

All judicial matters are decided according to *Shari'a* (Islamic law), not a written legal code.[17] Interpretation of the *Shari'a* is the exclusive jurisdiction of the Council of Senior *'Ulama*, the highest religious body in the country. The Saudi legal system considers public flogging, amputation, and beheading applicable to both Muslims and non-Muslims residing in the kingdom.

A special religious police force called the *muttawa* is charged with ensuring strict enforcement of *Shari'a* regulations. *Muttawa* enter homes forcibly, searching for evidence of non-Islamic behavior and harassing and abusing perceived transgressors.

Christian groups and other human rights groups have documented cases of more than one thousand Christian expatriates living and working in Saudi Arabia who have been arrested and imprisoned since 1990 for participating in private worship services. However, numerous incidents go unreported, especially among Egyptians, Indians, Koreans, Filipinos, and other Third World workers who fear reprisals against those arrested or family members still in Saudi Arabia.

According to Amnesty International, the persecution of Christians has "increased dramatically" in Saudi Arabia since the Gulf War.[18] In February 1996 Amnesty told a congressional hearing that hundreds of men, women, and children have been summarily arrested and ill-treated by the religious police—mostly without formal charges or trials—for the nonviolent expression of their religious beliefs. It is predominantly expatriate workers on short-term residence permits who are targeted by the religious police for activities such as the formation of clandestine worship groups.

In December 1995, seven Indian nationals were arrested and imprisoned in the kingdom for conducting a private Christmas service, reports Christian Solidarity International (CSI). The entire congregation of seventy was initially detained on December 22 near Dahran airport. According to CSI, the seven Indian nationals were abused in prison, with two being severely beaten. Three Filipino Christians were detained and imprisoned in Riyadh in October 1995.

In 1992, Filipino Christians Oswaldo Magdangal and Renato Posedio were scheduled to be beheaded on Christmas Day for holding secret Christian services. After an international outcry and a public appeal from Philippines President Fidel Ramos, King Fahd commuted their death sentence to an immediate deportation order.

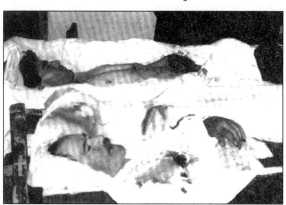

FIGURE 3–9
Christian father and son, Gevrije and Sami Bulut, were tortured and martyred by Muslim extremists in their home in Turkey in 1990. *Credit: International Christian Concern*

FIGURE 3-10

Iran's tiny Protestant community was devastated in 1994 by the brutal murders of three key pastors. The first to be killed was prominent evangelical pastor Haik Hovespian-Mehr (top), who launched an international campaign in 1993 on behalf of fellow pastor Mehdi Dibaj (bottom). Dibaj was imprisoned on death row on apostasy charges for converting from Islam to Christianity decades earlier. Dibaj was unexpectedly released from death row in January 1994, but Hovespian-Mehr disappeared a few days later. Authorities informed Hovespian-Mehr's family that he had been murdered by unknown assailants. On June 24, 1994, Dibaj himself disappeared. While Dibaj's fate remained unknown, Presbyterian minister Tateos Michaelian, who had replaced Hovespian-Mehr as head of the Protestant Council, was also mysteriously murdered. Three days later, on July 5, Iranian police announced that they had discovered Dibaj's murdered corpse "while searching for the killer of [Michaelian]". Terror struck the Christian community again in October 1996. The body of a fourth prominent leader, 34-year-old Assemblies of God pastor Mohammad Bagher Yusefi, was found hanging from a tree in a wooded area near his home in northwest Iran. A convert from Islam, he was close to the other murdered pastors and cared for Debaj's children. The murders have yet to be fully explained by authorities. *Credit: Compass Direct*

Magdangal has since moved to Chicago where he pastors an evangelical church. In a recent interview with *Christianity Today* magazine, he agreed that persecution has grown worse for Christians since his deportation. "[Saudi officials] want to prove they are in control," he said. "It has intensified now that they know the world knows about the persecution."[19]

The Saudi government has even made demands on the United States, restricting Christian worship by American citizens on U.S. embassy grounds in Saudi Arabia. American officials have apparently capitulated to some of these demands by restricting Christian services at the embassy in Riyadh and prohibiting displays of Christianity by U.S. troops defending Saudi interests during the Gulf War.[20]

EGYPT

Christian convert Hanaan Adel Rahman Assofti, who became a Christian more than five years ago, was arrested at Cairo's international airport in 1992 just before

boarding a plane to leave Egypt for good. During her detention she was interrogated for hours about other Muslim converts. She was eventually released into the custody of her parents, who were warned that they would be held accountable if Assofti maintained contacts with Christian groups or churches. The thirty-year-old woman is kept under virtual house arrest by her family.

Assofti is a woman without an identity in her homeland of Egypt. Security police confiscated her passport and identity papers in 1992 and never returned them to her—even though Egyptians are required by law to carry their personal identity card at all times. She has been told by police that she is "blacklisted" or forbidden to travel abroad—all because she left Islam to become a Christian.

In Egypt, new identity cards are issued for Christians who convert to Islam, but those such as Assofti who convert from Islam to Christianity are refused the same right. Although the Egyptian Parliament ratified international accords guaranteeing freedom of

FIGURE 3–11

Hanaan Assofti has been kept under house arrest in Egypt since 1992 because she converted to Christianity. This 28-year-old woman is on an official blacklist stating that she has no right to leave the country. Shortly after she became a Christian, she was arrested by police at the Cairo airport on her way to join her fiancee abroad. She is now forced to take Islamic instruction and is forbidden to have a Bible. She has received various death threats from Muslim extremists since her arrest. *Credit: NNI/Chris Woehr* religion, under the principles of *Shari'a* (Islamic law), Muslims who convert from Islam to another faith are regarded as "apostates" by the government, police, and courts.

Assofti occasionally manages to speak with other Christians. She says she feels continual social pressure to renounce Christianity. She is given a regular supply of books about Christians who have converted to Islam, and she has received frequent calls from Islamic sheikhs.

Throughout Egypt, converts from Islam to Christianity suffer severe persecution, including arrest, torture, and social ostracism. U.S. and Egyptian Christians working with the converts also face harassment, arrest, and expulsion. Egyptian Christians reported in 1995 that security police harassment, interrogation, and detention of Muslim converts to Christianity had increased significantly.

Rev. Keith Roderick, an Episcopal priest who directs the Coalition for the Defense of Human Rights under Islamization, explains: "During the last ten years, the government of Egypt has grown aggressive toward Christian converts by summarily detaining them under the Emergency Powers Act of 1982, torturing them, and—most insidiously—advocating that this 'religious problem' be taken care of by the family members of the converts who often impose an even more severe form of punishment."[21]

In one of the most prominent cases, Egyptian Christian convert Sharaf el-Din was imprisoned without trial in Cairo from October 1994 until June 1995. He was accused of "insulting Islam" and "giving false information" about Islam while he was living in Kenya.

FIGURE 3–12

Marzina Begum is a farmer's wife from Bangladesh who converted to Christianity in 1993 along with her husband and three children. During the Islamic season of Ramadan, Muslim mobs tried to force the family to observe the holiday; when they refused, the mobs beat her husband and broke his legs, stole their two cows and threatened to forcibly take her as a wife for a village leader. She fled into hiding. *Credit: Voice of the Martyrs*

The charge of "denigrating Islam" is regularly leveled against Muslim converts and Egyptian Christians involved in a Muslim's conversion.[22] He was finally released after a flurry of international diplomatic intervention in his case.

Members of Egypt's historic Coptic Christian community, representing about 10 percent of the population of sixty million, face pressures as well. In recent years, Islamists have increasingly targeted minority Christian communities for extortion and violence. Until recently—with the exception of Muslim converts to Christianity—the large Christian minority was left in peace. Now Islamic radicals are successfully forcing a greater Islamization of society.

The independent Egyptian magazine *Roz al-Yousef* tracked a sharp rise in the number of attacks by Muslim extremists against Christians, particularly those living in Upper Egypt. Six Christians were murdered in February 1996 by Muslim militants in the predominately Coptic area of Assuit Province.

"It appears that the killings were on account of religion," said Amnesty International in a statement condemning the murders.[23] Security officials blamed the attack on members of the militant *Gama'a al-Islamiya* group, which is waging a violent campaign to replace Egypt's government with a strict Islamic state.

In July 1996, two Coptic grocers in the Abu Qirqas region of Upper Egypt were gunned down in their shop by members of the radical *Gama'a al-Islamiya* group. Residents of the town say that many local Christians had received death threats over the previous eighteen months.

FIGURE 3–13
Fagu Miah, photographed with his wife, converted to Christianity along with his children and others from their farming community in Bangladesh. They were attacked by Muslim mobs during Ramadan. The 48-year-old farmer was beaten, his home was destroyed and his property was stolen. The family was forced to flee.
Credit: Voice of the Martyrs

Many Christians living in Upper Egypt have been pressured to pay "protection money" to Muslim racketeers.[24] According to Compass Direct, those who refuse have been subjected to violent attacks. In October 1995, Christian farmer Shehata Fawzi was shot to death after he refused to pay five thousand Egyptian pounds (about $1,500 in U.S. currency) to local Muslims. The Cairo-based Center for Human Rights/Legal Aid reports the murders of dozens of Copts over the past several years. The government has failed to put a stop to it.

In February 1996, a mob of some ten thousand Muslim youth pillaged and burned three Christian villages located in the Nile Delta approximately 60 miles northeast of Cairo. According to Compass Direct, the only response from the government was to provide a blanket and the equivalent of $7 to each affected family.

"Since the attacks in Upper Egypt started, tens of thousands of Christians have tried to escape the violence by migrating to Cairo. If they cannot flee, they convert to Islam to escape persecution," one writer in the region told News Network International.[25]

Violence has also erupted over church buildings. Under Egypt's ancient Hamouyony Decree, any church must have the express permission of the head of state—now President Hosni Mubarak—before building or making even minor building repairs. In late February 1996, police arrested fifty people in northeast Sharkiya Province after Muslim villagers rioted over a rumor that a local church would be expanded. In 1992, an Upper Egypt church was demolished for repairing its toilet without permission.

FIGURE 3–14
Hafizur Rahaman and his wife, also Christian converts, were similarly persecuted by Muslim mobs from their Bangladesh village. Mobs beat Rahaman so severely that he suffers permanent hearing loss in his right ear. They also stole his rickshaw, depriving him of a livelihood.
Credit: Voice of the Martyrs

Islam has been declared the state religion and *Shari'a* (Islamic law) has been the primary source of legislation in Egypt since 1980. Though Mubarak has resisted the total incorporation of *Shari'a*, its influence is increasingly felt. Simultaneously, Christian persecution has been on the rise, with converts to Christianity suffering the most abuse.

NIGERIA

The leaflet that was mass-distributed to Christians in Nigeria's predominantly Muslim state of Kano in 1995 was both ominous and explicit: "This is to inform you that for your interest and life security, you are seriously advised to pack out of Kano metropolis with immediate effect, otherwise your life will be in danger. And for your information, no authority can protect you from whatever calamity that may befall you if you fail to comply."[26]

The threat was especially potent because the leaflet, written by the Islamist group *Ja'amatu Tajudidi Islamiya*, was delivered in the wake of a new round of Muslim-Christian violence in Kano that had left one Protestant pastor dead and several Christian churches burned to the ground.

While the rise of a new militant Islam has been well documented in North African nations such as Algeria and Morocco, Christians in sub-Saharan states are reporting new attacks and threats as the Islamist movement spreads southward. A group of twenty-four African nations met in the Nigerian city of Abuja in 1989 and formed a new Islamic body called "Islam in Africa." According to a statement from the meeting obtained by News Network International, one of the key purposes of the group is to "eradicate in all its forms and ramifications all non-Muslim religions in member nations."[27]

FIGURE 3–15
A church building of the Evangelical Churches of West Africa was burned by Muslim extremists in Zaria, Nigeria.

Nigeria, Africa's most populous nation with one hundred million inhabitants, has seen countless interreligious clashes resulting in the death of approximately six thousand people—most of them Christian—since the early 1980s. In the nation as a whole, both Christians and Muslims say they are in the majority, but there are no census figures on religious affiliation. Muslims dominate many areas of the North, while Christians are the majority in the South. Christians have engaged in communal violence, though much of this appears to be defensive.

Northern Nigeria in particular has been an interreligious powder keg since the late 1980s. "Religious tensions between the northern Muslim-dominated part of the country and members of the Christian minority in the north have ignited several riots and attacks on Christians, resulting in scores of deaths and hundreds of injuries," reports Amnesty International.[28]

The situation in Kano state has been particularly tense since late 1994 when an ethnic Igbo Christian from southern Nigeria was brutally killed by Muslim extremists. The Christian, Gideon Akaluka, had been accused of desecrating the Koran, but a local court did not find sufficient evidence to convict him. Local sources reported that outraged Muslims stormed the prison where Akaluka was being held and beheaded him on the spot. His head was hoisted on a pike and paraded around the city.

New Muslim-Christian riots broke out in the area in late May 1995 (at least thirty people were killed) and again in mid-June after the Protestant pastor was murdered. Over the past two years about a dozen churches have been burned. In an apparently unrelated incident, an Irish Roman Catholic missionary nun was attacked and murdered in the southern Delta State in April 1995.

The nation's Roman Catholics have strongly condemned the ongoing military rule of General Sani Abacha, asserting that Nigeria "would have been better off if the military never intervened in the country's political affairs."[29]

Many Christians have complained that the government has moved too slowly in addressing the religious riots. "It seems the government is dragging its feet, but we won't relent in our efforts at providing security for ourselves and seeing justice prevail," said a representative of the Christian Association of Nigeria in an interview with News Network International.[30]

After a series of religious riots last year, Christians and Muslims began to form vigilante security groups in some areas of northern Nigeria in response to threats of more violence. Christians in the extreme north limited their movement and speech in some areas so they would not antagonize their Muslim neighbors. "The tension there is very high," a Nigerian Christian told News Network International.[31]

According to Compass Direct, a Christian preacher was kidnapped by members of a radical Shiite Muslim sect in September 1996 while preaching in a parking lot in the town of Kafanchan. A Christian and one of the kidnappers were killed in a forceful attempt by the Christian community to free him.

FIGURE 3–16
Congregation members sit in the burned sanctuary of their church, destroyed by a fire set by Muslim mobs in Nigeria. The church now meets under a tree.
Credit: Voice of the Martyrs

FIGURE 3–17
Christian Mrs. Malo Garba, photographed with her husband, has had two surgical operations to reconstruct her face after Muslim fanatics in Nigeria beat her—breaking all her teeth—for refusing to recite from the Koran. *Credit: Voice of the Martyrs*

Compass Direct also reports that in August 1996 government authorities in Kwara State closed three Christian schools—the Union Baptist Chapel School, the Baptist Model School, and Ogele Community Secondary School—because they did not include "Islamic Religions Knowledge" as part of their curriculum.[32] The closures are a setback to attempts by the churches to regain control of their schools seized by the government twenty or thirty years ago. The secretary general of the ecumenical Christian Association of Nigeria for Kwara State, Olusola Ajolore, denounced the government for dictating how schools funded exclusively by churches must operate.

FIGURE 3–18
Soner Onder, now 22 years old, has been incarcerated in a Turkish security prison for four-and-a-half years. He testified that he is not guilty of charges by Kurdish separatists that he participated in a firebombing attack in Istanbul in 1991. The young Christian testified at his trial that he was attending Christmas mass at his church during the attack, and was arrested off a public bus in a general police sweep after the incident. The police report declared that he was apprehended at the attack scene. Onder's testimony was supported by the local Syrian Orthodox Church prelate, as well as the driver of the bus. One policeman who signed his official arrest report even admitted under oath that he had not been at the scene nor had he arrested the teenager; he simply signed the report when told to do so. Christians connected to the Syrian church have been persecuted in recent years in Turkey. *Credit: NNI/B. Baker*

Religious tension is affecting American missionaries as well. An American Bible missionary had his passport confiscated by officials upon his arrival at Lagos International Airport in late 1996 and was unable to leave the country for several days, though no specific charges were leveled against him. The issue of religion was raised during interrogation by Nigerian authorities who were Muslim. It remains to be seen if this case marks the beginning of an ominous new pattern against foreign Christian visitors.

UZBEKISTAN

When the Berlin Wall came crashing down in 1989, there was great international optimism that the long era of religious repression in the former Soviet empire had come to an end. In many nations there has been dramatic improvement in religious liberty and human rights.

However, in the lower southwestern corner of the one-time Soviet stronghold, democracy, lingering communism, and a resurgent Islamization struggle for the heart of Central Asia. Nowhere is that battle more pronounced than in the Republic of Uzbekistan.

The most populous state in Central Asia, Uzbekistan is the acknowledged Islamic capital of the region. According to a U.S. Institute of Peace study, about 68 percent of the Uzbek population is Sunni Muslim, although one-quarter of the population claims to be "nonreligious."[33] Less than 5 percent of the population is Christian, and most are Slavic, Korean, or other immigrant minorities. Western groups estimate that there are only several hundred Uzbek Christian converts who meet together in small church groups.

Christian groups working in Uzbekistan in 1996 reported an increase of security police harassment of both Western Christian workers and Uzbek Christians. According to the international ministry Open Doors with Brother Andrew, Uzbek secret police officials have kept Uzbek believers under close surveillance. Several Christians have been detained and interrogated. One Uzbek convert to Christianity told Open Doors that secret police officials launched a pressure campaign to force him to recant after he became a Christian.

The government of President Islam Karimov, a former Communist Party leader, has adopted several policies to restrict religion—especially Christianity. Although the Uzbek Constitution guarantees freedom of conscience and religion, the government has prohibited "missionary activities" in an ambiguous 1991 law that fails to define such activities.[34] Proselytism is prohibited in an attempt to avoid religious tensions even though the constitution declares that citizens can "profess and spread their faith."[35]

Christian literature and films made in the Uzbek language may not be produced or distributed. Several church registrations have been revoked or denied. Three churches in Tashkent were ordered closed in June 1994. Uzbek officials cited a previously unknown law that religious meetings could not be held in public buildings. In December 1994, registration was revoked from the Word of Faith evangelical church because of its missionary work. In 1995, several smaller Christian ministries were also forced to stop operations. According to Compass Direct, Uzbekistan's secret police renewed their crackdown on Christians in the capital in September 1996, arresting the pastor of the Word of Faith church and fining him about $30 (the equivalent of three month's salary) for violating Article 241 of the Administrative Code, which forbids the teaching of religious beliefs without permission from the state's Department of Religion. The Pentecostal Church in the Fergana Valley was similarly harassed, and two members of the Baptist Union were taken to the security office and threatened with death by a general public prosecutor for their missionary activities; before being released, they were ordered to sign a statement promising to stop all Christian activities.

Karimov has used nominal Islam to shore up his government's legitimacy, although he has at the same time clamped down against Muslim extremists hoping to establish a militant Islamic state.

FIGURE 3–19

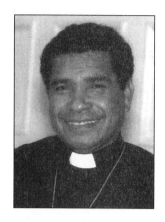

Roman Catholic Bishop Carlos Felipe Ximenes Belo of East Timor was awarded the Nobel Peace Prize in 1996 for his work in defending the religion and culture of the people of East Timor. In 1975, Indonesia—the world's most populous Muslim nation—invaded Catholic East Timor, and an esti- mated one-third of the population of East Timor lost their lives in the resulting war, terror, starvation and epidemics. As occupier, Indonesia has relentlessly repressed the East Timorese and has begun resettling Muslims to East Timor to dilute it's Christian culture. At the risk of his life, Bishop Belo has been the foremost representative of the people of East Timor. He has tried to protect the people from human rights abuses—including religious persecution—and has urged a just and non-violent settlement with Indonesia based on his people's right to self-determina- tion. Bishop Belo gained wide international recognition when he wrote a letter to the United Nations in 1989 Calling for UN-supervised referendum to bring peace to East Timor. "We are dying as a people and a culture," the Bishop stated. Christians in other parts of Indonesia also suffer persecution at the hands of Muslim fanatics, though not as systematic as that inflicted on East Timor. In October 1996, an evan- gelical pastor, his family and two others were burned to death in their church in East Java, Indonesia's most populous island. In a series of incidents beginning in June 1996, Muslim mobs destroyed eighteen Christian churches, two Christian schools and an orphanage in four cities in East Java. Churches targeted included those of the Baptist, Reformed, Pentecostal and Roman Catholic Churches. No group has claimed responsibility for the attacks which appeared to be coordinated, according to international press reports. *Credit: Arnold Kohen*

The Uzbek government tightened its restrictions in 1995 against the importation and printing of Christian literature by implementing a new "secret law" specifically aimed at Christianity. [36] According to Christian leaders in the Uzbek capital of Tashkent, local Christians were shown the text of the law by officials, but they were not allowed to make any copies of it.

Such a policy of secrecy was commonly used by the former Soviet regime, local Christians said, adding that it allows the Uzbek government to capriciously enforce the law or revise its application without public notice. A Christian leader who saw a copy of the law told News Network International that the code contained three stip- ulations, all designed to protect Muslim interests and restrict Christian materials.

KUWAIT

The following is a translation of Kuwait's Islamic court decision declaring Robert Hussein an apostate:

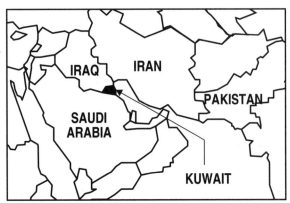

In the name of the Amir of Kuwait Sheikh Jabir Al-Ahmad Al-Jabir Al-Sabah we have reached a verdict.

Plaintiffs: *Abdulla Lafeef Al-Alsaleh*
       Mohammed Al-Jaddai
Defendant: *Robert Hussein*
29 May 1996

According to the motion papers and the court proceedings in which the Plaintiffs demanded the apostate conviction—which is beyond a reasonable doubt—and the convert declared to the Kuwaiti press that the Plaintiff is a Muslim citizen, and the desire to honor his religion is what motivated him to bring the charges against the Defendant.

By questioning the Defendant, he confirmed his apostasy from the Islamic religion after he was a Muslim, born to Muslim parents.

Both parties exchanged memorandum and the final adjudication of the court hearing is based upon the court's summary of the memorandum of the Plaintiff.

The summary of the Defendant's memorandum agreed with the Plaintiff's memorandum concerning the apostasy; however, the Defendant stated that the filed case was unconstitutional and the constitution allows the conversion.

According to the court decision:

First: The wise man is judged by his decision and he is the master of supreme evidence when he sees convincing evidence that the Defendant is guilty as charged. Not a shred of evidence came from the Defendant which would have prevented the imposition of the Shar'a Law against him. The plaintiff affirmed his apostasy in more than one location, both in front of the courtroom and publicly.

Second: According to his memorandum, the Defendant maintains that the court is incompetent to decide his case due to constitutional issues; however, the court finds that apostasy is covered in the constitution:

First: The defendant has a narrow point of view and does not clearly understand the provisions and articles of the constitution which focus on freedom of religion and its rituals. These constitutional freedoms stem from Mohammed's teaching. The constitution respects freedom of religion without fear of being closely monitored, but it does not mean that a Muslim should be allowed to convert from his religion to another. Everyone understands that there is a clear difference between these two points. However, the Plaintiff's claim was accurate, "If the case is elevated to the constitutional court it will not make any difference," because his conversion is absolute, and because he confessed by his tongue and by his actions. "The witness is his own testimony." He did not deny it. He stressed this more than once and he did not produce any new evidence to contradict the charges.

Second: What strikes the court are his indirect threats against the government, which should not come from a person whose strength stems from the bounty of this land of milk and honey. The government that you accuse is not a deaf Satan ("faroo"); watch out buddy!

According to what the Islamic scholars have emphasized regarding the convert by nature, the court agrees with the demands of the Plaintiff. The scholars know that there are two kinds of converts: F'tree: by nature and Miee

"F'tree": One who is born from two Muslim parents or at least one Muslim parent (like the defendant) and must be killed. In addition, his wife should be divorced from him and all his possessions be distributed to his heirs.

Among Muslim scholars there are plenty of examples of apostates being killed and there is no dispute.

Amar Al-Sabig said that Aba Abdulla said, "Any Muslim who converts from Islam and attacks Mohammed's prophecy and accuses him of being a liar, his blood should be shed. His wife should be divorced from him and his possessions should be distributed among his heirs and he should be killed. The Imam (ruler) should kill him without a chance to repent.

The court has ordered the following:

1. *The defendant is to pay all legal expense of this case according to Article 119.*

2. *The case will not be elevated to the constitutional court.*

3. *The defendant has been declared an apostate by nature.*

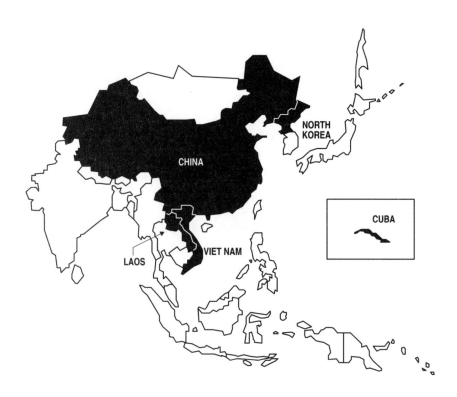

CHAPTER 4

Persecution in Communist Countries

CHINA

Thirty-one-year -old Huang Fangxin is a convicted criminal in China currently serving his prison sentence at a labor camp in Zhejiang Province. His crime? Being the "ringleader of an illegal religious organiza-

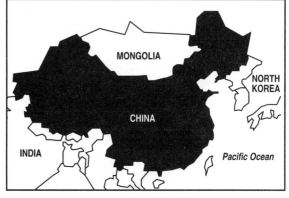

tion" that successfully converted many Chinese students to Christianity.[1]

Huang, a popular Protestant seminary student, left his studies at the government-sanctioned Jinling Union Theological Seminary in order to devote more time to his evangelistic projects. He recruited ten other young preachers to work with him in a "gospel team." But the team's success among Chinese youth made local officials uncomfortable.[2]

Arrested in early 1994, Huang was sentenced to three years of "reeducation through labor" for "disturbing the social order and normal religious life" and for "influencing the stability and unity of village life." Officials also accused him of being a "counterrevolutionary" and of collaborating with "hostile forces from abroad." While Huang currently languishes in labor camp, his church and colleagues remain under close police surveillance.[3]

Huang is not alone. In China today there are more Christians in prison because of religious activities than in any other nation in the world. Protestants are arrested and tortured for holding prayer meetings, preaching, and distributing Bibles without state approval. Roman Catholic priests and bishops are imprisoned for celebrating Mass and administering the sacraments without official authorization.

While China's closed penal system makes it difficult to obtain accurate numbers, Freedom House has a list of names of about two hundred Christian clergy and church leaders who were imprisoned or under some form of detention or restriction in mid-1996 because of religious activities. There are thought to be thousands of Christians now imprisoned for their faith in China's religious gulag. In several recent dragnet operations, hundreds of Christians were arrested. Some are serving sentences of up to a dozen years or more on "counterrevolutionary" charges, but the fact is they were incarcerated for practicing their faith.[4] Others are being held indefinitely—thrown behind bars by administrative decree without ever standing trial. Many Christian prisoners are forced to work in the *laogai*, the reform-through-labor camps where prisoners must toil as slaves for twelve hours a day, seven days a week, in automotive and chemical factories, brick-making plants, mines, and on farms. Chinese-American human rights activist Harry Wu has identified over one thousand prison work camps in the *laogai* system.

With the fall of the Iron Curtain, religious liberty improved dramatically in many Eastern European countries. But Christians and other religious believers living in countries still under the heavy hand of communism continue to face a hostile environment. In China, where estimates of the numbers of Christians range from fifteen million (government figures) up to one hundred million, religious freedom has been suppressed in varying degrees for over forty years—the situation is now particularly grave. While virtually all independent groups continue to experience oppression, Christians who resist government registration and control have been the largest single group in China proper facing a major deterioration in human rights. The Buddhists in Tibet have also suffered particularly severe treatment by the Chinese government in recent years.

FIGURE 4–1

One of China's best-known Protestant house-church leaders, Rev. Lin Xiangao (also known internationally as Pastor Samuel Lamb), is subjected to frequent interrogations, detentions and raids on his three-story house church in Guangzhou. The pastor has hosted meetings with hundreds of foreign visitors in his house, including U.S. politicians, human rights advocates and journalists. Because of his refusal to join the government-sanctioned Three Self Patriotic Movement which oversees Protestantism in China, he served twenty-one years in prison and labor camps. *Credit: Voice of the Martyrs*

The Chinese militantly suppressed Christianity from the mid-1950s until the 1970s when the Cultural Revolution ended, and many of the faithful spent decades in prison. The liberalizing trend that followed took a reverse course in 1989 when communism began to crumble in the Soviet empire and Chinese students rallied for democracy in Tiananmen Square. According to American Christians working in China, 1996 has been "the most repressive period" for Catholics and Protestants since the late 1970s.[5] "There has been a severe crackdown since the beginning of the 1996 calendar year," says David Stravers, executive vice-president of the Bible League, an evangelistic agency that supports Chinese churches.[6]

The mechanism for Beijing's control of religion is the Religious Affairs Bureau, controlled by the Department for a United Front, which itself is controlled by the Central Committee of the Communist Party. The Religious Affairs Bureau registers, oversees and controls all Christian churches within a framework provided by its Three-Self Patriotic Movement for Protestants and the Catholic Patriotic Association. Those with ultimate power for controlling religion in China are atheists—they are required to be so by Communist Party regulations. State religious policy, as explained by Chinese president Jiang Zemin in the March 14, 1996, edition of the *People's Daily*, is to "actively guide religion so that it can be adapted to socialist society."[7]

The Chinese are allowing the printing of Bibles, and Protestants and Catholics belonging to the state-sanctioned Patriotic

Associations are permitted to conduct religious activities, but only under very specific government regulations. Those straying outside the regulations risk swift government punishment. Catholics who choose to stay loyal to the Vatican and Protestant Christians who meet in unauthorized "underground" or "house" churches encounter severe persecution including fines, arrest, and imprisonment.

In January 1996, Chinese authorities renewed their drive to register all Protestant meetings. Though there are certainly many faithful Christians within the patriotic associations, millions of Chinese Christians have refused to seek government registration, believing that to register would compromise their faith by giving ultimate authority to the state rather than to God.

FIGURE 4–2
The father of these two Chinese children was jailed for distributing Christian literature. In China, the government restricts the production, importation and distribution of Bibles and other Christian publications. *Credit: Voice of the Martyrs*

Peter Yongze Xu, the leader of a house church with four million members, is one of those refusing to submit to government control. He has been in hiding since 1991 when he was released from prison after having been arrested while attending a service in Beijing led by American evangelist Billy Graham.

The registration campaign has been particularly aggressive in the city of Shanghai and the provinces of Anhui and Xinjiang. In 1996 hundreds of unregistered churches were raided and dozens of house-church Christians are still being arrested, detained, and fined. Over three hundred house churches in Shanghai were closed down in April alone. Reports from other provinces indicate new crackdowns as well. Compass Direct reports that five house churches were demolished near the town of Wenzhou, Zheijiang

FIGURE 4–3

Pastor Allen Yuan, photographed here with his wife, led a famous house church in Beijing until he felt compelled to close it in the fall of 1996 after police and officials from the Beijing Religious Affairs Bureau tried to force the 82-year-old evangelical to register the church with the government. Pastor Yuan's church in the capital and Pastor Lamb's church in Guangzhou are considered the two beacons of the unofficial house-church movement in China. In August 1996, Pastor Yuan baptized about two hundred converts. Millions of Chinese evangelicals have refused to register with the government, believing that registration would compromise their faith by giving ultimate authority to the state rather than to God. Those who resist registration risk fines, imprisonment and beatings. Allen Yuan has spent more than twenty years in prison for his faith. The text on the wall behind the couple in the photo reads, "Be thou faithful unto death, and I will give thee a crown of life, (Revelation 2:10)." *Credit: Voice of the Martyrs*

province, in May 1996. One of the most well-known house churches in the country—that of Pastor Allen Yuan in Beijing—was closed in fall 1996. The U.S.-based dissident journal *China Focus* quotes Pastor Yuan as saying, "We have only one room, and we don't even have any property, but the authorities still look at us as if we are monsters. All they want is to control us."[8] The popular pastor served twenty-two years in China's *laogai* for his faith.

The *Far Eastern Economic Review* reported in its June 6, 1996, issue that "police have destroyed at least fifteen thousand unregistered temples, churches and tombs" between February and June 1996 in Zhejiang province alone.[9]

Victims of the crackdown are legion. At least three evangelicals were killed by Chinese authorities during the first quarter of 1996, according to reports from the Voice of America and Compass Direct. One was Zhang Xiuju, a 36-year-old woman. On the night of May 26, 1996, she was dragged out of her home by police in Henan province and beaten to death. Police claimed that she had been killed while jumping from a car, but her family reported that when police delivered her body over to them, they offered the family six hundred dollars to keep quiet. A middle-aged man was beaten to death after being arrested near Wenzhou, Zhejiang province in April 1996. Two

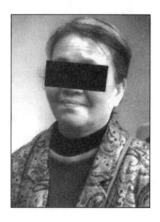

FIGURE 4–4
This Chinese evangelical woman, now in her sixties, is in hiding from police who seek her arrest for distributing Bibles. Voice of America and Compass Direct report that three evangelical Christians, including Zhang Xiuju, a 36-year-old woman, were beaten to death by police in early 1996 for reasons related to their Christianity. Many more Christians are serving prison terms in forced labor camps and other centers of detention. *Credit: Voice of the Martyrs*

men arrested with him were sentenced to three years of "reeducation through labor" and sent to the gulag. The three had been operating a printing press for religious materials. The third case concerns a twenty-four-year-old man in Shaanxi province who was one of ten beaten by police when they broke up a house-church meeting in April 1996.[10]

Another brutal incident occurred in March 1996 when five evangelical women were arrested and detained in western Xinjiang Province after a raid on a house church in a predominantly Muslim region. A total of seventeen church members were initially arrested, but twelve were released when the five women accepted responsibility for the gathering. Police severely beat several of the Christians, knocking out one woman's front teeth, and poured scalding water on those who resisted orders. The five women were imprisoned.

Catholics, too, have felt new pressures in 1996. Believers within the Roman Catholic Church are forced to affiliate with the government-sanctioned Catholic Patriotic Association, which does not recognize the ultimate earthly authority of the Pope. In 1958, the Chinese communist government began appointing its own bishops despite opposition from the Vatican.

The Connecticut-based Cardinal Kung Foundation reports that security troops conducted a series of raids in spring 1996 throughout the Baoding diocese in Hebei Province, which has a significant Catholic population. Priests—including two bishops—were arrested, churches were forced to register with the Catholic Patriotic

FIGURE 4–5
A destroyed Catholic church in Hebei Province, spring 1996.
Credit: Cardinal Kung Foundation

Association, and at least four thousand Catholics were forced to recant their faith publicly.[11]

The raids were apparently aimed at stopping participation in the annual May 24 Catholic pilgrimage to the village of Donglu in Hebei. Catholics had been coming to the site for a decade, and over ten thousand gathered in 1995 for a procession honoring Mary.[12] However, police crushed all commemorations in 1996. Clergy from the area were imprisoned or placed under house arrest, and some churches and prayer houses in the area were desecrated. One of two bishops arrested in February, An Shuxin, remains in detention in late 1996. [13]

FIGURE 4–6
Bishop Su Zhimin, the 64-year-old auxiliary bishop of Baoding, was arrested in a series of raids against Catholics in Hebei Province in spring 1996. Bishop Su had

already spent a total of fifteen years in prison because of his religious activities. Once he was beaten by security police until the board they were using was reduced to splinters. Not satisfied, the police then dismantled a wooden door frame in order to continue the beating, which soon splintered as well. On another occasion, the bishop was bound by the wrists and suspended from the ceiling while beaten. His head received numerous blows, causing permanent hearing loss. In still another prison episode, Bishop Su was placed in a closet-size room filled with water at varying levels, from ankle-deep to hip-deep. He was left there for several days, unable to sit or sleep.
Credit: Cardinal Kung Foundation

In a separate incident in March 1996 Bishop Zeng Jingmu, the seventy-six-year-old Roman Catholic Bishop of Yu Jiang, was sentenced without a trial to three years of "reeducation through labor" in the *laogai* for his religious activities after being arrested the previous November. Amnesty International reports that the bishop was accused by the Fuzhou Reeducation through Labor Committee of having "contravened regulations for supervising the registration of social organizations and, without registering, has organized group meetings at his home."[14] The bishop's life is reported to be in extreme danger due to a serious case of pneumonia he contracted during another prison stint earlier in 1995. He has already spent about two decades in the communist prisons for his faith.

In January 1996 Rev. Guo Bo Le, a Roman Catholic priest from Shanghai, was sentenced to two years of imprisonment at a "reform through labor" camp because of his "illegal religious activity."[15] He was arrested while celebrating Mass on a boat for about 250 fishermen. Guo's other "illegal" activities included administering the Sacrament of the Sick, establishing underground evangelical church centers, organizing catechetical institutes, teaching Bible classes and "boycotting" the Catholic Patriotic Association.[16] Fifty-eight-year-old Guo has already spent thirty years—over half his life—in Chinese communist prisons because of his faith.

Throughout 1996 the government arrested Catholic priests and nuns who offered Mass, distributed communion, and ran homes for the elderly and poor. Bishop Su Zhimin of Baoding—himself detained several times in the mid-1990s, having previously served a fifteen-year sentence for his faith—in a courageous letter to the National People's Congress Standing Committee dated June 15, 1996, protested: "The civil rights of the people, especially in the matter of religious worship, have been violated. . . . There is no way that the Roman Catholics can practice their religion routinely and normally."[17]

Foreigners are under tight restrictions in exercising their religious rights inside China. Decrees issued in recent years bar them from importing Bibles and religious tracts for distribution, evangelizing, establishing schools, and appointing religious leaders. Several foreigners, including some Americans, recently have been arrested, detained, or deported for practicing Christianity outside government control in China.

FIGURE 4–7
Tens of millions of Chinese evangelical Christians who worship in house churches are facing the worst government crackdown since the late 1970s.
Credit: Rev. Dennis Balcombe

Another cause for religious persecution stems from China's draconian one-child-per-family and eugenics-based population control programs. Those defying the strict population controls, including Christians motivated by conscience, are harshly punished by torture, imprisonment, fines, and forcible abortions and sterilizations. Several rural villages in Hebei Province were besieged in 1994, their inhabitants rounded up and collectively subjected to savage torture and property confiscations for giving birth to more children than the village quotas allowed.

Many Christian workers see little hope for improvement. One American Bible missionary who visited China in 1996 reported that an arrest warrant bearing the names of three thousand Protestant evangelical preachers is being circulated by the Chinese Public Security Bureau.[18]

In July 1995, communist hard-liner Ye Xiaowen was appointed to take charge of the Religious Affairs Bureau. In March 1996, Ye wrote an article in the Chinese publication *Renmin Ribao* describing his philosophy of "handling" religious affairs: "We must adopt an 'especially discreet,' 'very rigorous,' and 'circumspect' attitude toward these issues, as suggested by Lenin. . . . If, with a lapse of attention, they are not handled properly, it may undermine social stability, reform and opening up, and the overall interests of economic construction."[19]

Analysts such as Hong Kong-based evangelical preacher Rev. Jonathan Chao believe one motivation for the crackdown is the Communist Party's belief that Christianity, which continues to grow rapidly in the vast country, is the "principal threat" to China's political stability.[20] Beliefs such as the Christian tenet of individual human dignity remain anathema to communist officials who seek a monopoly on absolute political power.

• • • •

The following is a decision by a Chinese court in January 1996 that sentences Catholic priest Charles Guo Bo Le to two years in a labor camp for religious activities. He has already spent thirty years in Chinese prisons for his faith. It has been translated and provided by the Cardinal Kung Foundation.

THE PEOPLE'S GOVERNMENT OF SOOCHOW
PROVINCE OF JIANGSU
REFORM THROUGH LABOR MANAGEMENT COMMITTEE
REFORM THROUGH LABOR DECISION LETTER
No. 96–020

GUO BO LE, Christian name, Charles, male, age 58, Shanghainese.
Race: Han
Education Standard Attained: High School
Work Unit: Liaoyang Middle School, Yangou District of Shanghai,
(retired)
Current address: No. 6, 29th Section of Yangsi Town North Street,
Shanghai

Guo Bo Le was sentenced to five years' imprisonment as a counterrevolutionary in 1956 and was granted early release in March 1957. In July 1992, Guo was investigated by Changshou Public Security Bureau for involvement in numerous illegal religious activities. Subsequently, in September 1992, Guo was put on bail, awaiting trial by Shanghai Public Security Bureau. Again, on November 2, 1995, Guo was arrested by Wuxian City Public Security Bureau for conducting illegal religious activities and disturbing the order of the society.

The investigation revealed the following crimes:

> *Since November 1981, Guo Bo Le joined and has been active in the "underground" Catholic Jesuit secret organization, and received theology instruction. From 1990, Guo has visited Wuxian City, Xiang City, Taiping, Weitang, Changshou, Xu City, Xinzhuang, and Yangyuan districts, etc., and carried out illegal evangelical work: offered Masses, administered Sacrament of the Sick, administered other sacraments, promoted and supported the Roman Pontiff, instigated the people, boycotted the Patriotic Association, established illegal "underground" evangelical "church" centers, organized "underground" catechism instructions and Bible classes for primary and high school students, thus seriously disturbing the normal religious and social order.*

In accordance with Code No. 2, Section 3 of People's Congress: "Decision on Escapees, and Crimes of Former Labor Camp Prisoners and Reform Detainers," it is now decided that Guo Bo Le be given two years of reform through labor.

If one disagrees with this decision, an appeal may be filed with the Management Committee within fifteen days of decision.

Seal:
Reform Through Labor Management Committee of Soochow
January 4, 1996.

NORTH KOREA

Less than fifty years ago the North Korean capital city of Pyongyang was nicknamed "Asia's Jerusalem" due to the strong influence of Christianity there.[21] Some two thousand

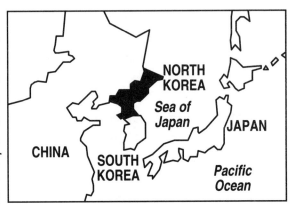

churches dotted the country's northern countryside, and Western missionaries were actively engaged in numerous projects. In 1948, communist dictator Kim Il Sung took power and began a systematic campaign of indoctrination in his own Stalinist ideology. Today, virtually all outward vestiges of Christianity have been wiped out, and North Korea is regarded as the most hard-line socialist nation in the world.

Kim considered Christianity to be "superstition" and "a hindrance to the socialist revolution."[22] By the early 1960s, his secret police had begun an intense effort against the faith. All church buildings were closed and all Bibles were destroyed. Clergy and religious leaders were either executed or sent to concentration camps.

In place of Christianity and other religions, Kim imposed an alternative religion—a personality cult, built around himself and his son, Kim Jong Il. From the time they are young children, North Koreans are taught to look on the "Great Leader" Kim Il Sung and Kim Jong Il as infallible, god-like beings and the progenitors of the Korean race.[23] The practice continues today, more than two years after Kim Il Sung's death.

Although some foreign observers have questioned whether Christianity still exists behind North Korea's tightly guarded frontiers, recent reports from Western missionary groups indicate that hundreds of thousands of North Korean Christians continue to cling to their faith despite nearly five decades of oppression.

Documenting human rights abuses in North Korea is extraordinarily difficult because it is one of the most closed societies in the world. The few Westerners permitted into the country are largely confined within the Pyongyang area where they are vigilantly supervised. The government's extremely tight security makes defections of North Korean citizens rare.

Still, according to several Koreans who have managed to defect, small groups of Christians continue to meet secretly in homes, although rarely in numbers larger than six. These "underground" Christians have no access to Bibles, religious literature, or teaching materials, according to Rev. Isaac Lee, the Seattle-based director of Cornerstone Ministries International.[24] Since North Korea is still closed to any kind of missionary work, most evangelistic projects are conducted clandestinely. Cornerstone Ministries is one of the few Western Christian groups that actively works inside North Korea.

North Korean officials insist that their constitution allows for religious freedom. The government operates three religious organizations: The Buddhist Federation, the Korean Christian Federation, and the Korean Catholic Association. The Protestant Korean Christian Federation claims to have ten thousand members, and the Catholic Association claims to have about three thousand members.

Since 1988, two Protestant churches and a Catholic church have been built in Pyongyang—three licensed church buildings for a nation of nearly twenty-five million. Although the churches have received widespread international publicity, several analysts believe they are merely government showplaces. Some visitors allege that the churches are only opened when foreign visitors request to attend services; others claim that the same church members appear to attend both the Protestant and the Catholic churches.

A *Washington Post* correspondent who attended services in two of the churches reported that the four Protestant congregants he was allowed to speak with could not name the first book of the Bible. Similarly, a British journalist met with a national leader of the Protestant federation who could not name the first three books of the Bible.[25]

In a 1995 interview with *Pyonghwa News*, a South Korea-based Catholic weekly newspaper, Chang Jae Chol, chairman of the government's Korean Catholic Association, asserted that about 250 of North Korea's three thousand Catholics regularly attend the church in

Pyongyang.[26] However, he acknowledged that—without an official priest—Catholics are unable to attend Mass or receive the Sacraments. North Korea has not allowed Catholic priests to be ordained since 1948.

Freedom of belief has no place in North Korea. The government relies on relentless propaganda and a comprehensive surveillance system to control virtually every act, thought, and desire of its citizens. North Koreans are prohibited from making even the slightest deviation from the Communist Party's rigid ideology.

VIETNAM

For Vietnamese Christian evangelist To Dinh Trung, the 1995 renewal of diplomatic and trade relations between the United States and Vietnam has made little impact on daily life. Trung is incarcerated in Vietnam's 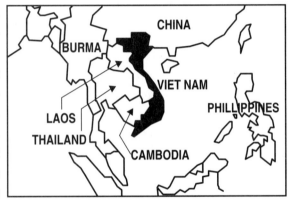 Quang Ngai prison where he has been sentenced to stay until 1998 for "abusing his freedom as a citizen by propagating religion illegally."[27]

Trung was arrested in April 1995, just as U.S. and Vietnamese officials were discussing normalizing relations two decades after the end of the Vietnam War. Trung, a worker in one of Vietnam's fastest growing Protestant house-church movements, was picked up while returning home on his bicycle after teaching a Bible lesson to ten people.

Normalization of U.S.-Vietnamese relations occurred in July 1995, while Trung remained in detention—still not officially charged with any crime. Finally, a "trial" took place on October 4, 1995.[28] According to witnesses, during the proceedings Trung attempted to defend himself before the judge, asking if his case had been handled in accordance with Vietnamese law. He told the judge he had been beaten during his incarceration, bound by hand and foot, and left to lie in the hot sun without water until he became delirious. The judge became angry and immediately pronounced Trung's sentence.

FIGURE 4–8 (LEFT)

Evangelist To Dinh Trung is imprisoned in Vietnam for "abusing his freedom as a citizen by propagating religion illegally." *Credit: Voice of the Martyrs*

FIGURE 4–9 (RIGHT)

This photograph, taken at great risk with a hidden camera, shows To Dinh Trung in a Vietnamese courtroom facing a communist judge in October 1995. When he questioned the lawfulness of the torture he received in prison, the judge became angry and sentenced him to three years of imprisonment for evangelizing. *Credit: Voice of the Martyrs*

Trung's wife wrote an eight-page letter of complaint to Vietnam's prime minister, detailing how existing law was consistently violated throughout her husband's arrest, pre-trial incarceration, trial, and imprisonment. Her efforts have been in vain, and Trung remains behind bars.[29]

FIGURE 4–10

To Dinh Trung's wife and children—the youngest only a year old—await his release from unlawful imprisonment. *Credit: Voice of the Martyrs*

71

FIGURE 4–11
Pastor Tran Mai, leader of a large evangelical house church that has branches throughout Vietnam, was arrested in 1991, probably because of his ties to foreign Christian groups. He was accused of "abusing religious powers and pursuing religious activities to fight the government." After being jailed without trial for more than a year, he was released in April 1993, possibly as an effort by Hanoi to cultivate goodwill with the United States in the period preceding negotiations on normalization between the two countries. *Credit: Voice of the Martyrs*

Despite Vietnam's highly publicized economic reforms and political overtures to the West, communist authorities continue to claim control over thought and belief in the Southeast Asian nation.

Following the diplomatic triumphs of 1995, the Vietnamese government embarked on a flurry of activity to intimidate and suppress independent worship. Both Protestants and Catholics have suffered. Because of the government's policy of secrecy surrounding its penal and detention systems, it is not known who and how many from Vietnam's Christian community are being punished for religious reasons at this time.

FIGURE 4–12
Vietnam singles out some of the most popular and successful Christian leaders for persecution. Pastor Nguyen Lap Ma, head of the Evangelical Church in Vietnam's

southwestern region, was forced from Saigon into internal exile in a remote rural village fourteen years ago. In 1992, he was placed under house arrest in the village where he remains without ever having had a court appearance or trial. He was declared by the government as the "number-one person against communism." His wife and ten children, pictured with him, join him in exile. *Credit: Voice of the Martyrs*

It is known, however, that a number of evangelical pastors have been detained and imprisoned, some Protestant churches shut down, many Bibles confiscated, ordinations to the Catholic priesthood sharply limited, and the appointment of a new Catholic bishop to the main Catholic diocese blocked.[30]

Vietnamese officials have also clamped down on unauthorized meetings between American and Vietnamese Christians. In February 1996, three Americans traveling with the evangelical group Youth with a Mission were placed under house arrest for several days after they were discovered singing hymns in a private home with twenty young Vietnamese Christians in Ho Chi Minh City. In September 1995, Vietnamese-American pastor Rev. An Doan Sauveur was arrested as he led an open-air service with seventy local Christians on a hillside outside Haiphong. He was then held three days under incommunicado house arrest before being fined and expelled from the country.

An American Christian with an Assemblies of God church in Sacramento, California is being detained in Vietnam for distributing pens with Christian crosses and audio tapes of Bible passages. Man Thi Jones, a 54-year-old naturalized American citizen who was born in Vietnam, was arrested on October 6, 1996 in her native village of

FIGURE 4-13
Pastor Ha Vvo La, shown below with his daughter and wife, has been a pastor for over twenty years with the K'Hor ethnic group of Vietnam. He has been imprisoned since 1995 for bringing the words of Christ to these tribal people. *Credit: Voice of the Martyrs*

Phan Rang (a tribal area of the Cham people that is located in south Vietnam) and charged with "religious propaganda" and related offenses. As this book goes to print, Mrs. Jones has been subjected to police interrogation on a near daily basis for over six weeks and has been placed under house arrest for over two weeks. She is being pressured to sign a confession of criminal activity and pay a fine. After first treating the Jones' situation as a routine criminal case, in response to appeals from human rights activists the U.S. State Department now states it is planning to protest Vietnam's denial of basic religious rights to the American citizen.

FIGURE 4–14
Christians pray in an illegal house church in Vietnam. In much of Vietnam, the government denies permission to establish churches, forcing believers to congregate illegally for prayer in private homes or makeshift churches. *Credit: Voice of the Martyrs*

The most brutal tactics appear to be used in remote areas outside the international spotlight. Among evangelicals the most severe pressure has been concentrated against ethnic tribal groups such as the Hmong, Hre, Koho, Jeh, and Jerai tribes. Local officials have been deeply concerned about the rapid growth of evangelical Christianity among these groups. According to a central highland pastor from the Koho tribe, the government views Christianity's strong appeal among tribal groups as a potential danger to Hanoi's authority in the highland regions. Tribal Christians report frequent arrests, threats, surveillance, and harassment by authorities. In May 1995, two Protestant evangelicals—Tran Van Vui and Nguyen Van Loi—were sentenced to two years of imprisonment in connection with their itinerant evangelizing among the Hre tribe. Three others were arrested for the "crime" of evangelizing on their bicycles and were denied food for five days for praying while in prison.[31]

Outside tribal areas evangelicals face restrictions as well. Although many pastors were released from long-term detention during the debate leading up to the lifting of the U.S. trade embargo, there has been a wave of new arrests since U.S. normalization. At least thirteen Vietnamese evangelicals are serving between two- and three-year prison sentences for attempting to spread Christianity. Harassment of Christian churches has taken other forms as well, such as short-term detentions, fines, and property confiscations. Unauthorized Protestant house-church leaders are currently subjected to staggering fines for holding prayer meetings and Bible studies.

Evangelicals do not have access to a new print-run of Bibles—the first legal Bibles allowed in several decades—unless they submit to the control of the government by registering their churches. Bibles belonging to citizens and tourists alike are routinely confiscated in Vietnam. In July 1995, Saigon airport authorities confiscated six hundred Bibles being brought in by American tourists.[32] In January 1995, police raided Village No. 3 of Son Nhat, confiscated all eight Bibles possessed by the thirty-five-member Christian community there, and prohibited them from holding house-church meetings.

Raids on independent evangelical churches are common. For example, in September 1995, authorities in Dalat raided a local

FIGURE 4–15
Catholic priest Father Dominic Tran Dinh Thu, founder of Vietnam's popular Congregation of the Mother Coredemptrix, was released from prison in a goodwill gesture to the United States in May 1993 after serving six years of a twenty-year sentence. In his eighties at the time of his arrest, he and twenty-two other priests and monks from his congregation were convicted with him at a mass show-trial for "propagandizing against the socialist system, sabotaging the solidarity policy, [and] disturbing public security and terrorism." It appears their real "crime" was their involvement in teaching adult religion classes. Twelve of those arrested in 1987 remain in prison. While most of the congregation has fled into exile and regrouped in Missouri, Fr. Dominic and several others decided to remain in Vietnam to bear witness to Christ. *Credit: Congregation of the Mother Coredemptrix*

FIGURE 4–16

Ho Van Loc, To Dinh Trung and Dinh Quang have been imprisoned since 1995 in Vietnam's Quang Ngai prison after they were caught evangelizing a 100-kilometer area which they covered on bicycles. They are in forced labor prisons, digging, chopping wood and cooking for the prison police. When they defied prison orders against praying, they were deprived of all food for five days. *Credit: Voice of the Martyrs*

FIGURE 4–17

Several Christians are serving time for their faith in Vietnam's Quang Ngai prison, above. There they are forced to do hard labor and forbidden to pray. Credit: Voice of the Martyrs

church affiliated with Rev. Dinh Thien Tu's house-church movement, the largest autonomous Protestant church in Vietnam. In August 1995, police even raided and closed a government-sanctioned church—the Baptist church in Dalat—after finding "illegal" Christian literature on the premises.[33] In August 1996, eleven churches in Ho Chi Minh City reported being raided by police, with entire congregations being detained for short periods.

Since the early 1990s, Vietnamese authorities have been putting severe pressure on the hierarchy of the Roman Catholic Church. The government has barred the appointment of a bishop to the key diocese of Saigon and has sharply restricted who and how many can graduate from the seminary and be ordained as priests. All religious activities must receive prior government approval.

In a petition to Vietnam's prime minister presented in September 1995, the Vietnam Catholic Bishops' Conference alleged that government policies have "seriously hindered our pastoral ministry and our faithful's religious life."[34]

The harshest persecution of Catholics continues to be directed against the popular Congregation of Mother Coredemptrix, the only order founded by Vietnamese Catholics. About a dozen priests and monks from the order have been imprisoned since 1987. Seventy-year-old Brother Nguyen Chau Dat, for example, is serving a twenty-year sentence on charges that he is a "counter-revolutionary" after his order was caught conducting catechism classes for adults.[35]

"No pen will ever be adequate to describe all the acts of terrorism, repression, suppression, murder and imprisonment aimed at the religious leaders and their followers—purely on religious grounds—in Vietnam," says Rev. Tran Qui Thien, a Catholic priest who spent thirteen years in a communist "reeducation" camp because of his religious activity.[36]

Much of the repression appears to be rooted in the government's view of Christianity as a threat to the communist regime. In Vietnam, authorities have coined the term "peaceful evolution" to describe the threat they feel from Christianity, which they perceive as a Western religion (Hanoi also harshly suppresses independent Buddhism to the point where the entire independent Buddhist leadership is in prison at the time of this writing).[37] The ruling Communist Party announced a harder line on religion at the 8th Party Congress in June 1996; authorities fear belief in Christianity undermines their absolute political and ideological control.

CUBA

Three days after his arrest on February 14, 1994, Baptist pastor and youth leader Eliezer Veguilla was ordered by state security police to "confess" to espionage or "sleep with a bear" that night.[38] When he resisted the interrogators' attempts to elicit a false confession, the 36-year-old Veguilla was roughly pushed into a dark, subterranean cell at police headquarters in Havana, only to find himself face-to-face with a live bear.

Terrified, he accepted the martyr's fate and—crouched in the corner of the cell—began to pray. As his eyes adjusted to the dim light, Veguilla realized that the bear was chained to the wall and could not reach him. This was yet another in a series of psychological torture tactics and death threats that he would endure over forty-seven days in the Cuban prison system, where he remained until international pressure forced his release.

"They couldn't tolerate my leadership among the youth, the large following that I was drawing into the many *casas culto* (house churches) that I had started," Veguilla says about the government. "Authorities would give me permission to preach to three hundred, and when a thousand showed up instead, they were angry. My

FIGURE 4–18
Baptist pastor Eliezer Veguilla was arrested in 1994 by Cuban police because of his success in evangelizing young people. During his detention he was forced to spend the night in a cell with a live bear.
Credit: Puebla Program on Religious Freedom

FIGURE 4–19

Pentecostal evangelist Orson Vila says his incarceration in a Cuban prison was not a punishment but a new opportunity to preach about his faith. The popular pastor, superintendent of more than eighty Assemblies of God fellowships, was arrested in May 1995 and sentenced to twenty-three months in prison for holding church services in his backyard. "I would never shut a church which Jesus Christ had opened," Vila told Compass Direct news service. Since communist authorities severely restrict the construction of new churches, numerous Cuban Christians such as Vila are forced to worship in private homes. Vila was "conditionally released" in March 1996 after an international protest over his case and sentenced to eight months under house arrest. *Credit: Voice of the Martyrs*

success in rallying young people for Christ was the real reason I was arrested," comments Veguilla from his home in Miami (where he is currently in exile).[39]

Like thousands of other Christian leaders, Veguilla sought refuge outside his homeland in late 1995. After his arrest—even though he had never been before a judge or received a trial—he was placed under house arrest for an indefinite period of time. He felt that it had become dangerous, not only for himself, but also for the other Christians who came to visit him. During prison interrogations he was shown videotapes of his religious meetings and services—even those he had attended during a short visit to the United States—proving that police agents were monitoring his activities. The Cuban government treated him as a terrorist and subversive solely because of his status as a Christian leader.

His father, Leoncio Veguilla, remains in Cuba as General Secretary of the Cuban Baptist Church and rector of the Baptist Theological Seminary of Havana. The elder Veguilla spent seven years in prison during the late 1960s when Cuba was a militantly atheistic state, simply for being a Christian; he now must walk a fine line within the present climate of limited religious tolerance.

Nearly forty years after Fidel Castro's communist revolution, religious freedom for both Catholics and evangelicals remains suppressed in Cuba. In 1960—the year after Castro seized power—all Christian broadcasting was summarily canceled. The next year, the production of all Christian publications came to a halt following the Bay of Pigs invasion. Catholic, Protestant and nondenominational schools were closed. By the end of the year, 3,500 priests, nuns and preachers had fled or been forced from the island. This marked the beginning of a decade of severe repression, during which ordinary Christians and their leaders were labeled "social scum" and jailed (Among those imprisoned in Cuba's notorious labor camps was a young Catholic priest, Jaime Ortega, now a Cardinal and the Archbishop of Havana).[40] Religious services were obstructed or disrupted, church property was vandalized, and educational and job opportunities were blocked for believers. Even American Voice of the Martyrs director Tom White spent years in Cuban prisons for distributing religious literature.

School children were ridiculed for their belief in God. Christmas and Easter were abolished as officially recognized holidays in 1970, subsequently replaced by secular observances honoring the heroes and accomplishments of the revolution. In 1976, the Cuban constitution was amended to outlaw religious beliefs opposing the revolution. Two years later, the Cuba Communist Party platform supported the "progressive elimination of religious beliefs through scientific-materialistic propaganda."[41]

In pre-revolutionary Cuba, 85 percent of the populace were baptized as Catholics. By 1989, this figure was only a fraction of one percent.

By the late 1980s, the darkest days of persecution seemed to be over. Christians are no longer afraid to go to church, and the churches are full—even flourishing. Christian churches are allowed to train and educate their leaders. Bibles are again distributed; in fact, the Bible was the best-selling title at the International Book Fair in Havana in both 1992 and 1993, reports Shawn Malone of Georgetown University's Center for Latin American Studies.[42] Open Doors reports an unprecedented tolerance of the importation of a record number of Bibles during 1996.[43]

In 1986, the Catholic Church sponsored the National Catholic Ecclesiastical Encounter, the first nationwide Catholic gathering held in Cuba since 1959. Other religious meetings have been permitted since then, including those with co-religionists abroad, though these meetings are closely monitored and sometimes infiltrated by police. According to the Christian news service Compass Direct, an estimated 1,500 Baptist youths from all over the island gathered for worship and evangelism in mid-1996.[44]

Since 1991, the Catholic Church—within strict limits and frequent setbacks—has been allowed to carry out social and humanitarian functions through *Caritas Cuba*, which now receives or oversees roughly 75 percent of all medical aid to the country.[45] The government undoubtedly saw this program as an opportunity to fill dire needs created by the collapse of Cuba's patron, the Soviet Union.

Nevertheless, Castro's communist dictatorship continues to impose many restrictions on religion, occasionally singling out Christian leaders like Pastor Veguilla for harsh persecution. Prohibitions on open-air meetings and public evangelism remain in effect; all worship must be confined to church buildings. Media access is—with few exceptions—typically denied, since the state forbids religious radio and television broadcasts. Christians are often discriminated against in both school and the workplace, despite a 1992 amendment to the constitution making such discrimination illegal. Jehovah's Witness and Seventh-Day Adventist groups are also banned.

Voice of the Martyrs and Open Doors reports that dozens of the approximately ten thousand evangelical house churches across the island were destroyed or shut down over the past two years, including Baptist, Assembly of God, Evangelical League of Cuba and Free Baptist Convention churches.[46]

In May 1995, Pentecostal pastor Orson Vila, superintendent of more than eighty Assemblies of God fellowships, was arrested and sentenced to nearly two years in prison for holding church services in his backyard. Under international pressure, Vila's punishment was shifted to eight months of house arrest beginning in March 1996.[47] Dozens of Christian leaders continue to report being interrogated and receiving threats on their lives.

Cuba's Catholic bishops have begun to speak out in recent years about the need for national reconciliation and a dialogue in which all

Cubans can participate. The government, however, has repeatedly told the bishops to "stay out of politics."[48]

Mainline Protestant churches—many of which have whole-heartedly supported the existing political and social structures—have fared somewhat better, according to Georgetown's Malone.[49] However, they have used their political favor only to lobby for space to carry out social projects.[50]

The uneven and unpredictable treatment of the churches by the Castro dictatorship in recent years creates its own pressures for Cuban Christians—especially the leaders—who never know when they might be penalized or if their churches will be crushed for becoming too bold, too popular or too secure. Nevertheless, nearly 41 percent of the population today are Catholic, and almost 3 percent are Protestant; both churches continue to grow.

LAOS

Christian leaders in the landlocked Southeast Asian nation of Laos were cautiously optimistic in early 1994. It seemed that new economic and political openness in the communist regime was leading to a period of openness for the repressed church as well. Catholic and Protestant churches were growing, and authorities had granted unprecedented approval for the printing of new Bibles.

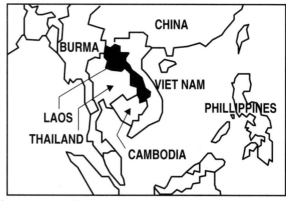

By year's end, however, optimism turned to anxiety. Word had filtered down from the northern province of Luang Pragang that local authorities were conducting seminars to inform rural villagers about government and Communist Party policies regarding religious activities. According to Christians who attended the meetings, officials used the seminars as an occasion to discredit Christians. Church members were accused of wrongdoing and told that their religious beliefs ran contrary to communist ideology.

FIGURE 4–20
All church buildings in Northern Laos were closed by the communists in 1975. This church in Luang-Prabang has been closed for twenty-one years. It has been taken over by the police, who now use it for their headquarters. No church is permitted in this city of about fifty thousand. *Credit: Voice of the Martyrs*

The practice continued throughout 1995 and expanded to other provinces. Many Christians attending the seminars were forced to sign an affidavit entitled "Regarding Ceasing the Activity of the Christian Religion"[51] The following is a translation of one such document obtained by News Network International:

> Having attended the seminar which studies the documents stating the line of the [Communist] Party and the government, I recognize that my beliefs are incorrect and are not in keeping with the Party and government line. I verify I will not have any interaction with the national Christian Committee in Vientiane [the name given to the national leadership of the Lao Evangelical Church].[52]

Signatories to the affidavit also agreed not to propagate their religious faith, attend church, or pray for divine healing when sick. Hundreds of Christians were persuaded or intimidated into signing the affidavits.

By the end of 1995 all known Protestant and Catholic churches in three northern provinces were forced to cease operations.

Veteran Indochina observers say the campaign against churches appeared to be part of a government attempt to bolster communist loyalty by fostering a greater sense of nationalism among the people. The nationalistic drive has been closely linked to Buddhism, which claims to represent about 60 percent of Lao society. Church leaders say there are more than thirty thousand Christians in Laos. Many of the government seminars were held in areas where Christianity has been growing rapidly among various ethnic groups.

Lao Christians say the harshest tactics of the campaign appear to have halted, though fear remains. A statement from the Mekong Prayer Fellowship, based in Thailand, said that churches in northern Laos are slowly trying to reorganize: "In some cases, Christians who were forced to give up their faith and church attendance have been able to gather in their churches again. In other places, they are meeting in small home-based groups. But some people are too afraid to get together at all."[53]

At least one Protestant pastor, Aroun Voraphom, remains in prison because of his religious activities. He was arrested in early 1996 and imprisoned in Bourikhamsay Province on several charges, including showing a video without permission, "causing division," and illegally "spreading his faith."[54]

"Implementation of [Communist] Party/government policy in Laos has always been contextualized to local provincial situations. Consequently, in some areas the Christian church is suffering more than in others," said the Mekong Prayer Fellowship statement.[55]

Protestants and Catholics throughout the country are uneasy about the future. Catholics were prohibited in 1995 from commemorating the hundredth anniversary of the founding of a local Catholic mission in southern Laos, despite the fact that government officials had given prior approval for the celebrations. According to the Hong Kong-based Union of Catholic Asian News press service, local authorities denied permission for the event just three days before the ceremonies were due to begin. The mission was one of the first Catholic settlements established along Asia's Mekong River.

One Indochina expert who visited Laos in May 1996 reported that many church leaders fear the campaign in the North may have been "a 'pilot project' by the authorities which is now being evaluated and will likely be repeated in other places."[56]

According to local press reports, communist leaders told delegates at a February 1996 meeting of the Lao Front for National Construction that, while in the past the "number-one enemy of the people" was the United States, today their primary enemies are Protestant Christians and the Baha'i—the two fastest-growing religious groups in the country.[57]

CHAPTER 5

Call to Action

WHILE THE RECENT PAST HAS BEEN largely marked by silence and indifference to the persecution of Christians, there are signs that the tide is now turning. More and more Christian leaders are vowing to give new priority to the issue.

The movement began in full force on January 23, 1996, when more than one hundred key Christian leaders and activists gathered in Washington, D.C., at a consultation convened by Freedom House to discuss strategies for mobilizing a new activism about the global persecution of Christians. Among those in attendance were Richard Land of the Southern Baptist Convention; Chuck Colson of Prison Fellowship Ministries; Don Argue of the National Association of Evangelicals; D. James Kennedy of Coral Ridge Presbyterian Church; Joseph Stowell of Moody Bible Institute; Gary Bauer of the Family Research Council; Ravi Zacharias of Ravi Zacharias International Ministries; Peter Torry of Open Doors U.S.A.; Keith Roderick of Coalition for the Defense of Human Rights under Islamization; Drew Christiansen of the U.S. Catholic Conference; George Weigel of Ethics and Public Policy Center; and Carl Anderson of the Knights of Columbus.

Participants heard details about the persecution faced by Christians in China, Sudan, Pakistan, Saudi Arabia, Vietnam, and elsewhere, and they discussed strategies for ensuring that persecution issues receive more attention in U.S. foreign policy.

"You have seared my conscience today, and I don't think I'll ever be able to forget this issue," said Colson at the conclusion of the meeting. "But am I able to sustain it day in and day out, and continue to try to educate the people who are within my sphere of influence? That is our challenge."[1]

85

At the meeting, the National Association of Evangelicals (NAE) released a *Statement of Conscience* expressing "deep concern for the religious freedom of fellow believers, as well as people of every faith."[2] The statement invited other religious groups to "join us to work tirelessly to bring about action by our government to curb worldwide religious persecution."[3]

"We are dismayed that the United States government has been indifferent to its obligation to speak out against reigns of terror now being plotted and waged against Christians. At the same time, we confess our own culpability in failing to do all within our power to alleviate the suffering of those persecuted for their religious beliefs," the NAE *Statement of Conscience* stated.[4]

At the Southern Baptist Convention annual meeting in June 1996, delegates voted to endorse the ideas expressed in the NAE *Statement*. Some mainline Protestant groups are also supporting the document. The Executive Council of the Episcopal Church has voted to express its "support in principle" of the NAE *Statement*, and commissioners to the Presbyterian Church (U.S.A) denominational meeting in New Mexico in July 1996 also officially voted to commend NAE for the statement.[5]

Catholic leaders are speaking out as well. In his annual speech to the Vatican diplomatic corps in January 1996, Pope John Paul II raised the issue of religious persecution, singling out China, Vietnam, and several Islamic countries. The persecution of Christians is "an intolerable and unjustifiable violation, not only of all the norms of current international law, but of the most fundamental human freedom, that of practicing one's faith openly, which for human beings is their reason for living," the Pope said.[6]

"When Episcopalians, evangelicals, Southern Baptists and Roman Catholics are all voicing grave concerns over the persecution of Christians in other countries, I believe we can say that 'critical mass' has been reached," asserts Richard Land.[7]

Since the January Freedom House consultation, Colson and several other Christian leaders have been meeting to discuss follow-up strategies for translating concern about persecution to action from grassroots Christians in the pews. Christian media outlets including

Christianity Today magazine, the popular "Focus on the Family" radio broadcast, Christian Broadcasting Network, the television broadcast of D. James Kennedy, Chuck Colson's "BreakPoint" column, and the Catholic Eternal Word television broadcast have devoted time and space to discussing the persecution of Christians.

In an editorial in the *Washington Post* entitled "Human Rights for Christians Too," prominent columnist Stephen Rosenfeld described the new activism on Christian persecution, calling it "the most intriguing early foreign policy development of 1996 in Washington."[8] He wrote, "Until now, [persecution of Christians] has not been embraced as a generic global phenomenon requiring a focus and strategy of its own."[9] He concluded his editorial: "Politically as citizens and objectively in terms of the pain of foreign brothers, the Christian community has right and reason to be heard. The effort will save lives."[10]

Organizers of the new movement believe a successful public campaign on behalf of persecuted Christians can be modeled after the campaign for Soviet Jewry, when both Christians and Jews worked together to eliminate persecution.

"A focused campaign against these persecutions supported by a committed domestic constituency—such as sensitized and informed American Christians—can, and we believe will, have tremendous and far-reaching results," Land says.[11] "The American campaign on behalf of Soviet Jews helped to seal the fate of Soviet repression in its far-flung empire.[12] We believe a campaign to use American governmental influence to stop the persecution of Christians may well have similarly dramatic results."[13]

On September 29, 1996, thousands of evangelical churches throughout the United States observed an "International Day of Prayer for the Persecuted Church." The occasion, designated as such by the World Evangelical Fellowship, was organized by a loose coalition of activist and church associations including the Southern Baptist Convention, the National Association of Evangelicals, Prison Fellowship Ministries, Campus Crusade for Christ, the Assemblies of God Church, Ravi Zacharias International Ministries, Coral Ridge Ministries, the Lutheran Church-Missouri Synod,

Moody Broadcasting Network, the Institute for Religion and Democracy, Freedom House, and numerous others. Packets of educational materials and prayer suggestions for Christian communities that are suffering under oppression were mailed to seventy thousand evangelical pastors throughout the country. Though largely unreported by the secular media, thousands upon thousands of ordinary American Christians were introduced to the tragedy unfolding against their brothers and sisters in faith in many parts of the world.

Advocates say there are many avenues for action, from high-profile publicity efforts to diplomatic negotiations to letter-writing campaigns. One increasingly important strategy may be using economic influence. "The fact that we are now a global society means that we can put pressure on countries because we have things like global trade that countries depend upon," says Christopher Catherwood.[14] "You can use trade and other economic factors as leverage. The fact that there is a global economic system probably helps persecuted Christians—if people in the Western wealthy industrialized countries actually use the economic leverage they have."[15]

Overall, U.S. government leaders need to take a stronger moral stance on the issue. "The main thing is for American civil society to be aroused and for many private groups to be active in international affairs. Such private groups as Amnesty International and Freedom House have had a great effect in real world politics, even when they did not have much support from the government," states Michael Novak of the American Enterprise Institute. "But," Novak stresses, "our government, too, in its foreign policy could be much more conscious of the religious dimension of persecution and oppression."[16]

"It is the responsibility of governments to defend religious freedom for their citizens. And it is our government that can best speak to other governments, either bilaterally or through multilateral organizations, especially the UN," argues Diane Knippers, president of the Institute on Religion and Democracy. "It is this possibility of U.S. government action, in fact, which is one of the best avenues to empower U.S. citizens and church-goers to address this issue at all."[17]

In its *Statement of Conscience*, the NAE urged several "achievable goals" for the U.S. government, including a major policy address by the president; the appointment of a special adviser to the president for religious liberty; improvements in State Department research and documentation of religious liberty violations; changes in what the NAE called the "indifferent and occasionally hostile manner" in which the Immigration and Naturalization Service treats religious asylum cases; and termination of nonhumanitarian aid to countries that allow religious persecution.[18]

"We are not insisting that the U.S. government seek to hold the entire world to the pristine standard of the U.S. Constitution's First Amendment religious liberty rights and guarantees, as desirable and as beneficial to humankind as we believe that would be," Land emphasizes. "We are insisting that basic human rights be recognized."[19]

There are some early hopeful signs that American political leaders are beginning to respond to the mounting outrage by the American Christian community about the treatment of Christians abroad.

In the first half of 1996, shortly after Christian leaders met in Washington to discuss how to deal with the global problem of persecution against Christians, congressional committees held four hearings where the topic of persecution of Christians was addressed. In February the House Subcommittee on International Operations and Human Rights—chaired by longtime religious liberty advocate Rep. Chris Smith (R-NJ)—held the first hearing in its history that focused exclusively on the plight of persecuted Christians abroad.

On September 17, 1996, the United States Senate unanimously adopted a resolution stating that many foreign Christian communities "are restricted in or forbidden from practicing their faith, victimized by a 'religious apartheid' that subjects them to inhumane, humiliating treatment, and in certain cases are imprisoned, tortured, enslaved, or killed." The resolution states that, "unfortunately, the United States has, in many instances, failed to raise forcefully the issue of anti-Christian persecution at international conventions and in bilateral relations with offending countries." It "strongly recommend[s]" that President Clinton "expand and invigorate the United States' international advocacy on behalf of persecuted Christians, and initiate a thorough examination of all United States' policies that affect persecuted Christians."[20] A similar resolution was unanimously adopted by the

House of Representatives a week later.[21] Both resolutions, though having the support of the entire Congress, are nonbinding.

After pulling back from an initiative to appoint a special advisor to the president on religious freedom, the administration announced in late 1996 that it was forming an advisory committee to report to the secretary of state on issues relating to religious liberty. The committee is comprised of members with various religious affiliations and interests. What impact the committee will have on administration policy in the area of persecution against Christians remains to be seen.

But congressional hearings and resolutions focusing on Christians under siege in many parts of the world and the formation of an advisory committee on religious freedom by the administration, however encouraging, must not be equated or confused with an actual change in American foreign policy. No actual change—or even an announced intention for change—in policy regarding Christians oppressed abroad has yet occurred. It is also important to remember that these initiatives grew directly out of the broader campaign by the Christian community. While there have always been individual members of Congress and the executive branch sympathetic to the plight of persecuted Christians, it is highly unlikely that even the modest steps taken—the nonbinding resolutions and advisory committee—would have occurred had it not been for the grassroots support and leadership of many prominent Christian churches and ministries throughout 1996.

The U.S. needs to once again send the message to the world that our citizens care deeply about religious freedom—that religious freedom, in fact, is what animates our republic. There needs to be explicit concern raised for the millions of persecuted Christians around the world.

"America has great power and influence. Such power contains responsibilities as well as privilege," says Richard Land.[22] "We expect our government to insist that nations who want to be in good relation with us cease and desist from persecuting Christians.[23] A foreign policy that denies our basic values and seeks only to meet the requirements of commerce and business is, and will always remain, totally unacceptable."[24]

Christians Are
Compelled to Help

BY RAVI ZACHARIAS

CHRISTIANS ARE CALLED BY THEIR very belief in Christianity to help others who are persecuted for their faith. In the essay that follows, Ravi Zacharias, award-winning evangelical author, Christian radio broadcaster and founder of the Atlanta-based Ravi Zacharias International Ministries, establishes that the Gospels call Christians to take action on behalf of the persecuted—especially other Christians who are besieged for their faith.

• • • •

In 1934, Christian theologian Reinhold Niebuhr penned a prayer that would become one of the most quoted prayers of this century: "O God, give us the serenity to accept what cannot be changed, the courage to change what should be changed, and the wisdom to distinguish the one from the other." Today, the prayer is still repeated, but it is seldom applied. Allegiance to the idea remains, but the imperative contained in the idea is met with disregard.

The same danger now plagues the Church, even as she is experiencing one of the most painful wounds ever inflicted upon her. A cause of extraordinary magnitude awaits the cry and help of the Christian, but silence lurks where anguished voices should be heard. The issue is that of a tidal wave of persecution, of dehumanization, torture, and death carried out upon Christians in many parts of the world by hate-filled opposers of the Gospels.

The situations documented elsewhere in this book well describe the atrocities being committed against those who dare to follow

91

Christ. What is worse, such brutality is taking place while Western governments and individuals of influence turn a blind eye to these horrors, leaving Christian men, women, and children with no place to turn. The Bible makes a strong assertion that persecution for righteousness' sake will ever confront the Christian. But at the same time, it also solemnly charges us to take up the cause of the needy and to speak for those who are victims. The Scriptures challenge us to reach out to those who hurt, to do all in our power for the rescue of those who are victimized, and if need be, to beseech the powers of the land to give each citizen the right of being treated as a fellow human being.

In his letter to Timothy, Paul wrote to say how lonely it was when there was no one to help him in his persecution. Yet all too often, Christians, confident of an Eternal City, absolve themselves of any responsibility for the here and now.

To most in the West, recent history is forgotten. This disregard makes us forget the terrifying lessons even of this century, lessons we ignore at our own peril. If we do not speak up for those who are presently abused by lawless and criminal minds in the name of whatever they claim to believe, is it possible that such hate will grow unimpeded until it is at our own doorstep?

But there is indeed a greater call than that of self-preservation. The entire Book of Obadiah in the Bible is devoted to a people who stood on the sidelines and did nothing while their brother's land was plundered and his people raped. Obadiah tells us, "Because of the violence against your brother Jacob, you will be covered with shame; . . . On the day you stood aloof while strangers carried off his wealth and foreigners entered his gates," (vv. 10–11).

These Scriptures give us clear guidelines for addressing persecution. First and foremost, we are called to concerted prayer. When Peter and Paul were in prison, the entire church gathered to pray for their release.

Beyond the burden of prayer is the call to action. Jesus left the ninety-and-nine sheep to go look for the lost one. Action is also the moral imperative of the parable of the good Samaritan. In striking contrast to the priest who took the easy road of prayer alone, the

Samaritan stopped in his equally busy journey to extend the love of Christ to the wounded. The apostle Paul encouraged the Church of his time to take responsibility for the well-being of their fellow believers. "Therefore," he said, "as we have opportunity, let us do good to all people, especially to those who belong to the family of believers" (Gal. 6:10). This reaching out with love is part of the Gospels' imperative.

There is the precedent for appealing to the government for justice. In the Book of Acts, when the crowd wanted to lynch Paul, he laid claim to his Roman citizenship and demanded a hearing before Caesar. In our context, the National Association of Evangelicals' *Statement of Conscience* suggests several concrete ways we can urge our own government to take up the cause of our persecuted brothers and sisters. For indeed, these are our brothers and sisters who are dragged away from their homes, who are terrorized because of their faith. The stories are real, and their numbers are many. If your son or daughter, your husband or wife, your brother or sister were at this moment in prison, sold into slavery, or held by kidnappers simply because of their love for Christ, would you serenely accept it as something unchangeable, or would you show the courage to do all in your power to speak for them?

We live in an hour when Niebuhr's concerted prayer needs to be invoked in heartfelt earnest. May God grant us all the wisdom not only to pray for those who are wronged, but also to draw His strength to speak to others of that which must be made right. The silence of the many on behalf of the some will only breed evil that ultimately destroys us all.

NATIONAL ASSOCIATION
OF EVANGELICALS'

Statement of Conscience

The National Association of Evangelicals (NAE) released the following Statement of Conscience *at the Freedom House conference on the Global Persecution of Christians on January 23, 1996. In it the NAE, a membership organization of 42,500 congregations across the United States, takes note that "Evangelical Protestants and Catholics have become special targets of reigns of terror initiated by authorities who feel threatened by Christian faith and worship." The NAE pledges to "end our own silence in the face of the suffering of all those persecuted for their religious faiths" and "to do what is within our power to the end that the government of the United States will take appropriate action to combat the intolerable religious persecution now victimizing fellow believers and those of other faiths." The* Statement of Conscience *sets forth five principal steps the president of the United States should take to stop religious persecution abroad.*

The NAE Statement of Conscience *that follows has been endorsed or commended by the Southern Baptist Convention, the Episcopal Church, the Presbyterian Church U.S.A., and the United Methodist Church.*

· · · ·

FOREWORD

This *Statement of Conscience* of the National Association of Evangelicals reflects our deep concern for the religious freedom of fellow believers, as well as people of every faith. We invite others to join us to work tirelessly to bring about action by our government to curb worldwide religious persecution.

FACTS

The persecution of religious believers has become an increasingly tragic fact in today's world. In many countries, moreover, Evangelical Protestants and Catholics have become special targets of reigns of terror initiated by authorities who feel threatened by Christian faith and worship. Such authorities, often motivated by anti-Western, antidemocratic ideologies, also persecute Christians as a means of threatening the freedom of all persons subject to their authority. Incidents of religious persecution are legion:

- In many Islamic countries, where militant and xenophobic Islamist movements seek to capture the soul of a historically tolerant Islamic faith, and where the demonization of Christians also serves to intimidate Muslims seeking freedom from repressive regimes.

- In China, Cuba, Laos, North Korea, and Vietnam, where remnant Communist regimes feel threatened by persons whose Christian faith places them under an authority transcending governments, and where the persecution of Christians also serves to intimidate non-Christian dissenters.

- In other parts of the world, where persons of evil intent rightly understand that the survival of churches undermines their aims, because these churches affirm the human dignity of all persons created in God's image and acknowledge their ultimate accountability to a transcendent God.

- In countries and regions where the demonization of powerless Christian scapegoats often serves to vent, foment, and popularize hatred of the West and the United States.

- Imprisonment and torture of persons for simply attending Christian worship services or Bible studies.

- Establishment of government-controlled "religious associations" and criminal prosecution and torture of members of "unlicensed" Christian churches.

- Refusal to permit Vatican appointments of Catholic bishops and refusal to allow nonapproved bishops to appoint local priests.

- Encouragement and appeasement of unpunished mob violence against Christians conducting burial and other religious services.

- Encouragement and appeasement of unpunished looting and burning of businesses and homes of practicing Christians.

- Church burnings and systematic official refusals to allow the building of new churches or church repairs.

- Encouragement and appeasement of systematic beatings of children who attend Christian schools.

- Literal sale into slavery of Christian children abducted by government forces.

- Refusal to distribute food to Christians in famine-stricken areas unless they agree to renounce their faith.

- Wide dissemination, often with government support, of scurrilously hateful, deliberately provocative, anti-Christian tapes, books, and tracts.

- Imprisonment of Christians for the mere possession of Bibles. Prosecution, torture, and even murder of practicing Christians under infamous and broadly construed "blasphemy" laws.

- Prosecution, torture, and even murder of Christian converts and the children and grandchildren of such converts, under equally infamous and broadly construed "apostasy" laws.

PRINCIPLES

If people are to fulfill the obligations of conscience, history teaches the urgent need to foster respect and protection for the right of all persons to practice their faith.

If people are to fulfill the obligations of conscience, history cries out for an end to today's wrongful silence, by Christians as well as others, in the face of mounting persecution of Christian believers.

If governments are to be worthy of the name, or responsive to their national interests and the interests of their people, lessons of history mandate uncompromising hostility to religious persecution.

If, though it is true, the United States government cannot end all evil throughout the world, it can nonetheless adopt policies that would limit religious persecution and ensure greater fulfillment of inalienable and internationally recognized rights to freedom of religious belief and practice.

CALL TO ACTION

It is lamentable that persecution of religious believers is pervasive around the world.

We are dismayed that the United States government has been indifferent to its obligation to speak out against reigns of terror now being plotted and waged against Christians. At the same time, we confess our own culpability in failing to do all within our power to alleviate the suffering of those persecuted for their religious beliefs.

We know that the United States government has within its power and discretion the capacity to adopt policies that would be dramatically effective in curbing such reigns of terror and protecting the rights of all religious dissidents.

As a matter of conscience, therefore, we respectfully call for the following actions to be taken by the government of the United States:

I. *Public acknowledgment of today's widespread and mounting anti-Christian persecution and the adoption of policies condemning religious persecution whether it results from official policy or from unchecked terrorist activity.*

To that end, we respectfully recommend that the following steps be taken:

- A major policy address by the president initiating a new public diplomacy commitment to openly condemn anti-Christian persecution wherever it occurs and further announcing a lesser reliance on today's private diplomacy and case-by-case appeals to curb such persecution.

- Issuance of instructions to all ambassadors or surrogates to meet regularly with willing church leaders and dissidents in countries where religious persecution occurs.

- Appointment of a knowledgeable, experienced, and compassionate special advisor to the president for Religious Liberty charged with preparing a report indicating needed changes in policies dealing with religious persecution, and recommending remedial action.

- Issuance of instructions to the United States delegate to the United Nations Commission on Human Rights to regularly and forcefully raise the issue of anti-Christian and other religious persecution at all appropriate Commission sessions.

- Issuance of instructions to consular officials acknowledging the mounting evidence of religious persecution and instructing them to provide diligent assistance when the victims of religious persecution seek refugee status.

- Issuance of instructions to senior officials engaged in trade or other international negotiations, when dealing with officials of countries that engage in religious persecution, to vigorously object to such religious persecution, and to link negotiations with the need for constructive change.

II. *Issuance by the State Department's Human Rights Bureau and related government agencies of more carefully researched, more fully documented, and less politically edited reports of the facts and circumstances of anti-Christian and other religious persecution.*

To that end, we respectfully recommend that the following steps be taken:

- Issuance of instructions to human rights officers to distinguish between the treatment of different Christian groups within countries and no longer to assume that all such groups are similarly dealt with.

- Issuance of instructions that Human Rights Bureau annual reports are to make explicit findings of whether anti-Christian or other religious persecutions occur, thereby eliminating from such reports any "option of silence" regarding such persecutions.

- Clarifying and upgrading the role of embassy human rights officers in countries where anti-Christian or other religious persecution is ongoing and pervasive, and ensuring that such officers carefully monitor religious liberty violations on an ongoing and prioritized basis.

III. *Cessation of the indifferent and occasionally hostile manner in which the Immigration and Naturalization Service often treats the petitions of escapees from anti–Christian persecution.*

To that end, we respectfully recommend that the following steps be taken:

- Issuance of an Attorney General's Bulletin to INS hearing officers acknowledging mounting anti-Christian persecutions in many parts of the world, and directing such officers to process the claims of escapees from such persecution with priority and diligence.

- Issuance of instructions by the attorney general and the secretary of state directing preparation of annual INS reports describing its processing of religious refugee and asylum claims.

- Issuance of regulations requiring access to written opinions from INS hearing officers clearly stating the grounds for any denial of religious refugee and asylum claims.

- Establishment of INS listening posts in countries to which refugees from anti-Christian persecution frequently flee.

- Cessation of INS and State Department delegation of complete responsibility for refugee processing functions to international and United Nations agencies.

- Development and issuance of training guidelines for INS personnel on issues specifically related to religious persecution.

IV. Termination of nonhumanitarian foreign assistance to governments of countries that fail to take vigorous action to end anti-Christian or other religious persecution, with resumption of assistance to be permitted only after a written finding is made by the president that the countries have taken all reasonable steps to end such persecution, and arrangements are made to ensure that religious persecution is not resumed.

CONCLUSION

Religious liberty is not a privilege to be granted or denied by an all-powerful State, but a God-given human right. Indeed, religious liberty is the bedrock principle that animates our republic and defines us as a people. We must share our love of religious liberty with other peoples, who in the eyes of God are our neighbors. Hence, it is our responsibility, and that of the government that represents us, to do everything we can to secure the blessings of religious liberty to all those suffering from religious persecution.

We appeal not only to our own government, but to the governments of every nation that would be free, to treasure religious freedom. A people cannot be truly free where the elemental justice of religious freedom is abridged or denied. If justice is to "roll on like a river," religious persecution around the world must cease.

Therefore, before God, and because we are our brother's keeper, we solemnly pledge:

To end our own silence in the face of the suffering of all those persecuted for their religious faith.

To address religious persecution carried out by our Christian brothers and sisters whenever this occurs around the world.

To withhold assistance by our member denominations to those countries that fail to take action to end religious persecution.

To do what is within our power to the end that the government of the United States will take appropriate action to combat the intolerable religious persecution now victimizing fellow believers and those of other faiths.

Denominational Resolutions and Letters of Support

RESOLUTION OF THE SOUTHERN BAPTIST CONVENTION

ON CHRISTIAN PERSECUTION

JUNE 11–13, 1996

Adopted by: Messengers to the Southern Baptist Convention's Annual Meeting, June 1996

Whereas, vast numbers of Christians have experienced persecution and martyrdom in the twentieth century and because of their faith are now facing mounting reigns of terror throughout much of the world; and

Whereas, the Christian faith is restricted and, in some places, banned; and believers are imprisoned, killed, enslaved, or otherwise persecuted; and

Whereas, in many places throughout the world where the numbers of evangelicals are increasing or Christianity is newly spreading, Christian minorities face persecution and discrimination as scapegoats, often for the venting of popular hatred of the West and the United States; and

Whereas, the West is increasingly indifferent to the denial of religious freedom to millions of Christians worldwide; and

Whereas, religious liberty is a God-given human right, not a privilege to be granted or denied by the State; now, therefore,

BE IT RESOLVED, that we the messengers to the SBC, assembled in New Orleans, Louisiana, June 11–13, 1996, unwaveringly denounce the denial of fundamental human rights and all religious persecution anywhere in the world; and

BE IT FURTHER RESOLVED, that we urge President Bill Clinton, the State Department, and both houses of the United States Congress to uphold the fundamental freedom of religious liberty in the conduct of foreign policy by the United States of America; and

BE IT FURTHER RESOLVED, that we urge all Christian leadership to call Christians worldwide to fervent prayer for the constant protection and power of the Holy Spirit in the daily lives of all Christians everywhere who may be vulnerable to persecution; and

BE IT FINALLY RESOLVED, that we individually and collectively observe September 29, 1996, as International Day of Prayer for the Persecuted Christians.

CONCERNING WORLDWIDE RELIGIOUS PERSECUTION

ADOPTED BY THE
208TH GENERAL ASSEMBLY (1996)
PRESBYTERIAN CHURCH (U.S.A.)

Whereas, we are joined in Scripture to "remember those who are in prison, as though you were in prison with them" (Heb. 13:3, NRSV); and

Whereas, the General Assembly of the United Presbyterian Church in the United States of America declared in 1974 that "American Christians, who live under the mandates of the gospel and who share the rights and privileges of constitutional government and the freedoms attached thereto, must speak out to defend human rights everywhere"; and

Whereas, the General Assembly of the Presbyterian Church in the United States affirmed in 1978 that "because God is working for human rights and calls us to do so, we stand ready also to exert pressure on institutions, politics, and people"; and

Whereas, the freedom of conscience is among the most precious of human rights and among the most frequently violated worldwide; and

Whereas, the National Association of Evangelicals has issued a "Statement of Conscience Concerning Worldwide Persecution" calling attention to the widespread persecution of Christians and others around the world and pledging "to end our own silence in the face of the suffering of all those persecuted for their religious faith" and asking the U.S. government and others to take action aimed at curbing persecution; therefore, be it

Resolved, That the 208th General Assembly (1996) of the Presbyterian Church (U.S.A.):

1. Commend the commissioners for bringing this *Statement of Conscience* concerning worldwide religious persecution to the attention of the assembly and also commend the National Association of Evangelicals for their concern for religious liberty.

2. Reaffirm the long-standing commitment of the Presbyterian Church (U.S.A.) to religious freedom as identified in the following principles:

    a. History teaches the urgent need to foster respect and protection for the right of all persons to practice their faith if people are to fulfill the obligations of conscience.

    b. History cries out for an end to today's wrongful silence, by Christians as well as others, in the face of religious persecution.

    c. Governments, to be worthy of name and responsive to the interests of their peoples, must exercise uncompromising hostility to religious persecution.

3. Request that the issues of religious persecution, the *Statement of Conscience,* and related U.S. human rights and asylum policies be referred to the Worldwide Ministries Division, in consultation with the Advisory Committee on Social Witness Policy, for study and action, with a report and any other further recommendations to come to the 209th General Assembly (1997).

4. Urge General Assembly agencies to continue their cooperation with the World Council of Churches, World Alliance of Reformed Churches, National Council of Churches, and World Conference on Religion and Peace in their efforts to monitor and work to eliminate religious oppression and the misuse of religion for purposes of power.

5. Direct the stated clerk to communicate to the president of the United States and the secretary of state urging that the U.S. adopt and implement domestic policies that limit religious persecution and ensure greater fulfillment of internationally recognized rights to freedom of religious belief and practices.

RESOLUTION ON ENDORSING THE
Statement of Conscience

CONCERNING WORLDWIDE RELIGIOUS PERSECUTION

ADOPTED BY THE EXECUTIVE COUNCIL OF THE GENERAL CONVENTION OF THE EPISCOPAL CHURCH FEBRUARY 9, 1996

Resolved, that the Executive Council of the General Convention of the Episcopal Church expresses its support in principle of the *Statement of Conscience* concerning worldwide religious persecution in support of religious liberty as authored by the National Association of Evangelicals; and be it further

Resolved, that certified copies of the resolution be forwarded to the NAE, NCCC, Anglican Observer to the United Nations, President of the United States, and Episcopal members of Congress.

EXPLANATION

The Executive Council has been asked to join its voice with Evangelical and Catholic organizations in support of the cause of persecuted Christians around the world. The statement is similar in content, tone and intent to the Human Rights and Religious Liberty Statement adopted by the National Council of the Churches of Christ at its governing board meeting in November 1995.

The statement calls on the U.S. government to use its influence abroad. Specifically, the statement calls for:

a) a policy statement by President Clinton;
b) the appointment of a special advisor to the president on religious liberty;
c) improvements in State Department research and documentation of religious liberty violations;

107

d) change in the Immigration and Naturalization Services classification to recognize religious asylum;
e) termination of foreign aid to countries that allow religious persecution.

August 2, 1996
Ms. Diane Knippers, President
The Institute on Religion & Democracy
1521 16th Street, N.W., Suite 300
Washington, D.C. 20036

Dear Ms. Knippers:

You recently sent to the General Board of Global Ministries the "Statement of Conscience of the National Association of Evangelicals Concerning Worldwide Religious Persecution."
We are pleased with the contents of this document. As a member communion of the National Council of Churches of Christ in the USA, United Methodists have taken note of several areas of collaborative work with the NAE on issues of religious liberty. The two organizations developed and successfully implemented a joint strategy to gain passage of the Religious Freedom Restoration Act in the current U.S. Congress. They drafted guidelines for religion and public education in the U.S. They also worked on the appeal process for the Lamb's Chapel case gaining equal access to public school facilities for after-school use by religious groups.

You will be pleased to know that the General Board of Global Ministries is in full support of partner churches which face hostile and militant religious fundamentalism. We are supportive of Bishop Samuel Azariah of the Raiwind Diocese of the United Church of Pakistan, where he and other church leaders have risked arrest and prosecution under state *shri'a* laws for transporting Christians to safety in other countries. The General Conference heard a report from Bishop Peter Dabale of local conflicts and violent encounters with Muslim fundamentalists in northern Nigeria. We continue to support religious freedom for our restored United Methodist ministries and the rule of our missionaries in Eastern Europe, especially in countries where Communist leadership has been reinstalled and the control of religious activity is once again a popular political objective of state authority.

With these and other mounting challenges we are most pleased with all evidences of proactive support of the Christian community for protection of religious rights and liberty.

Sincerely,
Bishop F. Herbert Skeete
President, General Board of Global Ministries

Bishop Dan E. Solomon
President, World Division
General Board of Global Ministries
United Methodist Church

RESOLUTIONS OF
THE UNITED STATES CONGRESS

Senate Concurrent Resolution 71

SEPTEMBER 17, 1996

Whereas oppression and persecution of religious minorities around the world has emerged as one of the most compelling human rights issues of the day. In particular, the worldwide persecution and martyrdom of Christians persists at alarming levels. This is an affront to the international moral community and to all people of conscience.

Whereas in many places throughout the world, Christians are restricted in or forbidden from practicing their faith, victimized by a "religious apartheid" that subjects them to inhuman, humiliating treatment, and in certain cases are imprisoned, tortured, enslaved, or killed;

Whereas severe persecution of Christians is also occurring in such countries as Sudan, Cuba, Morocco, Saudi Arabia, China, Pakistan, North Korea, Egypt, Laos, Vietnam, and certain countries in the former Soviet Union, to name merely a few;

Whereas religious liberty is a universal right explicitly recognized in numerous international agreements, including the Universal Declaration of Human Rights and the International Covenant on Civil and Political Rights;

Whereas Pope John Paul II recently sounded a call against regimes that "practice discrimination against Jews, Christians, and other religious groups, going even so far as to refuse them the right to meet in private for prayer," declaring that "this is an intolerable and unjustifiable violation not only of all the norms of current international law, but of the most fundamental human freedom, that of practicing one's faith openly," stating that this is for human beings "their reason for living";

Whereas the National Association of Evangelicals in January 1996 issued a "Statement of Conscience and Call to Action," subsequently commended or endorsed by the Southern Baptist Convention, the Executive Council of the Episcopal Church, and the General Assembly of the Presbyterian Church, U.S.A. They pledged to end their "silence in the face of the suffering of all those persecuted for their religious faith" and "to do what is in our power to the end that the government of the United States will take appropriate action to combat the intolerable religious persecution now victimizing fellow believers and those of other faiths";

Whereas the World Evangelical Fellowship has declared September 29, 1996, and each annual last Sunday in September, as an international day of prayer on behalf of persecuted Christians. That day will be observed by numerous churches and human rights groups around the world;

Whereas the United States of America since its founding has been a harbor of refuge and freedom to worship for believers from John Winthrop to Roger Williams to William Penn, and a haven for the oppressed. To this day, the United States continues to guarantee freedom of worship in this country for people of all faiths;

Whereas as a part of its commitment to human rights around the world, in the past the United States has used its international leadership to vigorously take up the case of other persecuted religious minorities. Unfortunately, the United States has in many instances failed to raise forcefully the issue of anti-Christian persecution at international conventions and in bilateral relations with offending countries; now, therefore, be it

Resolved, that the Senate, the House of Representatives concurring:

(1) unequivocally condemns the egregious human rights abuses and denials of religious liberty to Christians around the world, and calls upon the responsible regimes to cease such abuses; and

(2) strongly recommends that the president expand and invigorate the United States' international advocacy on behalf of persecuted Christians, and initiate a thorough examination

of all United States' policies that affect persecuted Christians; and

(3) encourages the president to proceed forward as expeditiously as possible in appointing a White House special advisor on religious persecution; and

(4) recognizes and applauds a day of prayer on Sunday, September 29, 1996, recognizing the plight of persecuted Christians worldwide.

HOUSE RESOLUTION 515
SEPTEMBER 24, 1996

Whereas oppression and persecution of religious believers around the world has emerged as one of the most compelling human rights issues of the day; in particular, the worldwide persecution and martyrdom of Christians persists at alarming levels, and this is an affront to the international moral community and to all people of conscience;

Whereas in many places throughout the world, Christians are restricted in or forbidden from practicing their faith, victimized by a "religious apartheid" that subjects them to inhumane humiliating treatment, and are imprisoned, tortured, enslaved, and killed;

Whereas in some countries proselytizing is forbidden and extremist elements persist unchecked by governments in their campaigns to eradicate Christians and force conversions through intimidation, rape, and forced marriage;

Whereas in several Islamic countries conversion to Christianity from Islam is a crime punishable by death and an Islamic court in Kuwait has denied religious liberty to a convert from Islam to Christianity;

Whereas the militant Muslim government of Sudan is waging what its leader has described as a *jihad* (religious war) against Christian and other non-Muslim citizens in the southern part of the country, enforcing *Shari'a* (Islamic law) against non-Muslim African Sudanese, torturing, starving, killing, and displacing over 1,000,000 people, and enslaving tens of thousands of women and children;

Whereas today in Sudan a human being can be bought for as little as $15;

Whereas Christians in China are now experiencing the worst persecution since the 1970s;

Whereas there are more documented cases of Christians in prison or in some form of detention in China than in any other country;

Whereas both Evangelical Protestant house church groups and Roman Catholics have been targeted and named "a principal threat to political stability" by the Central Committee of the Communist Party of China;

Whereas in recent months, in separate incidents, three Chinese Christian leaders were beaten to death by Chinese authorities simply because of their religious activities;

Whereas 3 Christian leaders in Iran were kidnapped and murdered during 1994 as part of a crackdown on the Iranian Christian community;

Whereas severe persecution of Christians is also occurring in North Korea, Cuba, Vietnam, Indonesia (including East Timor), and in certain countries in the Middle East, to name only a few;

Whereas religious liberty is a universal right explicitly recognized in numerous international agreements, including the Universal Declaration of Human Rights and the International Covenant on Civil and Political Rights;

Whereas Pope John Paul II recently sounded a call against regimes that "practiced discrimination against Jews, Christians, and other religious groups, going even so far as to refuse them the right to meet in private for prayer," declaring that "this is an intolerable and unjustifiable violation, not only of all the norms of current international law, but of the most fundamental human freedom, that of practicing one's faith openly," stating that this is for human beings "their reason for living";

Whereas the National Association of Evangelicals in January 1996 issued a *Statement of Conscience and Call to Action*, subsequently commended or endorsed by the Southern Baptist Convention, the Executive Council of the Episcopal Church, and the General

114

Assembly of the Presbyterian Church, United States of America, in which they pledged to end their "silence in the face of the suffering of all those persecuted for their religious faith" and "to do what is in our power to the end that the government of the United States will take appropriate action to combat the intolerable religious persecution now victimizing fellow believers and those of other faiths";

Whereas the World Evangelical Fellowship has declared September 29, 1996, and the last Sunday in September each year thereafter, as an international day of prayer on behalf of persecuted Christians, and that day will be observed by numerous churches and human rights groups around the world;

Whereas, the United States of America since its founding has been a harbor of refuge and freedom to worship for believers from John Winthrop to Roger Williams to William Penn and a haven for the oppressed, and has guaranteed freedom of worship in this country for people of all faiths;

Whereas historically the United States has in many instances failed to intervene successfully to stop anti-Christian and other religious persecution; and

Whereas in the past the United States has forcefully taken up the cause of other persecuted religious believers and the United States should continue to intervene on behalf of persecuted Christians throughout the world; Now, therefore, be it

Resolved, that the House of Representatives:

(1) reaffirms its commitment to the Nation's historic devotion to the principles of religious liberty;

(2) unequivocally condemns the egregious human rights abuses and denials of religious liberty to Christians and other persecuted religions around the world and calls upon the responsible regimes to cease such abuses;

(3) strongly recommends that the president expand and invigorate the United States' international advocacy on behalf of persecuted Christians and other persecuted religions and initiate a thorough examination of all United States policies that affect persecuted Christians;

(4) encourages the president to take organizational steps to strengthen United States policies to combat religious persecution, including the creation of a special advisory committee for religious liberty abroad which has an appropriate mandate and adequate staff or to consider the appointment of a White House special advisor on religious persecution; and

(5) applauds the actions of the World Evangelical Fellowship in declaring an annual international day of prayer on behalf of persecuted Christians.

Selected Bible Passages Concerning Persecution and Prayer

"God created man in his own image" (Gen. 1:27–28).

"I was in prison," Jesus said, "and you came to visit me" (Matt. 25:36).

"Remember those in prison as if you were their fellow prisoners, and those who are mistreated as if you yourselves were suffering" (Heb. 13:3).

"I saw the tears of the oppressed—and they have no comforter" (Eccl. 4:1).

"He who oppresses the poor shows contempt for their Maker" (Prov. 14:31).

"If a man shuts his ears to the cry of the poor, he too will cry out and not be answered" (Prov. 21:13).

"Jesus replied: 'Love the Lord your God with all your heart and with all your soul and with all your mind.' This is the first and greatest commandment. And the second is like it: 'Love your neighbor as yourself.' All the Law and the Prophets hang on these two commandments" (Matt. 22:37–40).

"Rescue those being led away to death; hold back those staggering toward slaughter. If you say, 'But we knew nothing about this,' does not he who weighs the heart perceive it? Does not he who guards your life know it? Will he not repay each person according to what he has done?" (Prov. 24:11–12).

"Carry each other's burdens, and in this way you will fulfill the law of Christ" (Gal. 6:2).

"But God has combined the members of the body and has given greater honor to the parts that lacked it, so that there should be no division in the body, but that its parts should have equal concern for each other. If one part suffers, every part suffers with it; if one part is honored, every part rejoices with it" (1 Cor. 12:24–26).

Paul commends a friend because he "was not ashamed of my chains. On the contrary, when he was in Rome, he searched hard for me until he found me [in jail]" (2 Tim. 1:16b–17).

The lions in the den of the Babylonians were muzzled through the prayers of Daniel: "My God sent his angel, and he shut the mouths of the lions" (Dan. 6:21).

"The commander went to Paul and asked, 'Tell me, are you a Roman citizen?' 'Yes, I am,' he answered. . . . 'I was born a citizen,' Paul replied" (Acts 22:27–28).

"About midnight Paul and Silas were praying and singing hymns to God, and the other prisoners were listening to them. Suddenly there was such a violent earthquake that the foundations of the prison were shaken. At once all the prison doors flew open, and everybody's chains came loose" (Acts 16:25–26).

Endnotes

Introduction / It's a Crime to Be Christian

1. See pages 54–55 for complete text of Kuwait Religious Court Ruling, 29 May 1996.

2. Yossef Badansky and Vaughn S. Forest, "Islam Against the Church," Task Force on Terrorism & Unconventional Warfare, House Republican Research Committee, U.S. House of Representatives, 19 January 1994, 6–7.

3. Testimony of Richard Land, president, Christian Life Commission of Southern Baptist Convention, before the Committee on International Relations, Subcommittee on International Operations and Human Rights, House of Representatives, 15 February 1996.

4. Statement of Michael Horowitz, before Members' Briefing on Religious Persecution of the Congressional Human Rights Caucus, House of Representatives, 7 March 1996.

5. Stephen S. Rosenfeld, "Human Rights for Christians Too," *Washington Post*, 9 February 1996.

6. Telephone interview of Rev. Richard J. Neuhaus by Nina Shea, 11 October 1996.

7. See House Resolution 515, 24 September 1996, and Senate Concurrent Resolution 71, 17 September 1996. In their entirety, both are appended to this book.

8. See appendix, "Statement of Conscience of the National Association of Evangelicals Concerning Worldwide Religious Persecution," 23 January 1996.

9. Pope John Paul's Annual Address to Diplomatic Corps, 13 January 1996, Vatican Information Service, 15 January 1996.

10. Statement of Chuck Colson at Freedom House Conference on the "Global Persecution of Christians," 23 January 1996, Washington, D.C.

11. Ibid. See appendix, "Statement of Conscience of the National Association of Evangelicals Concerning Worldwide Religious Persecution," 23 January 1996.

Chapter 1 / Prolonged Silence of American Christian Churches

1. Telephone interview of Michael Novak by Nina Shea, 10 October 1996.

2. Interview of Christopher Catherwood by Kim A. Lawton, Prague, Czech Republic, 6 May 1996.

3. Telephone interview of David Stravers by Kim A. Lawton, 13 May 1996.

4. Telephone interview of Paul Marshall by Kim A. Lawton, 15 May 1996.

5. Ibid.

6. Ibid.

7. Ibid.

8. Interview of Reg Reimer by Kim A. Lawton, Prague, Czech Republic, 6 May 1996.

9. Telephone interview of Diane Knippers by Nina Shea, 4 October 1996.

CHAPTER 2 / WESTERN FAILURE

1. Testimony of Richard Land, president, Christian Life Commission of Southern Baptist Convention, before the Committee on International Relations, Subcommittee on International Operations and Human Rights, House of Representatives, 15 February 1996.

2. Telephone interview of Paul Marshall by Kim A. Lawton, 15 May 1996.

3. Telephone interview of Rev. Richard J. Neuhaus by Nina Shea, 11 October 1996.

4. Samuel Huntington, "The Clash of Civilizations," *Foreign Affairs,* Council on Foreign Relations (New York, New York), summer 1993, 22.

5. Statement of Michael Horowitz, before Members' Briefing on Religious Persecution of the Congressional Human Rights Caucus, House of Representatives, 7 March 1996.

6. Ibid.

7. Richard Land testimony, 15 February 1996.

8. Telephone interview of Michael Novak by Nina Shea, 10 October 1996.

9. Telephone interview of George Weigel by Nina Shea, 10 October 1996.

10. Meeting of Ambassador Jim Sasser with human rights nongovernmental organizations, attended by Nina Shea, U.S. Department of State, Washington, D.C., 24 January 1996.

11. Testimony of Nina Shea, director, Puebla Program on Religious Freedom, Freedom House, hearings on the U.S. State Department Country Reports on Human Rights Practices for 1995, before the Subcommittee on International Operations and Human Rights, Committee on International Relations, House of Representatives, 26 March 1996.

12. Michael Horowitz statement, 7 March 1996.

13. Testimony of Abe Ghaffari, president of Iranian Christians International, before the Committee on International Relations, Subcommittee on International Operations and Human Rights, House of Representatives, 15 February 1996.

14. Ibid.

15. Meeting of assistant secretary for Human Rights, Labor, and Democracy with nongovernmental organizations and scholars attended by Nina Shea, U.S. Department of State, Washington, D.C., 6 November 1995.

16. Interview of Wilfred Wong by Kim A. Lawton, Prague, Czech Republic, 6 May 1996.

17. Ibid.

CHAPTER 3 / PERSECUTION IN ISLAMIC COUNTRIES
SUDAN

18. Testimony of Dr. Kevin Vigilante, representative, Puebla Institute, before the Subcommittee on Africa, Committee on International Relations, U.S. House of Representatives, 22 March 1995.

2. Ibid.

3. Ibid.

4. Gaspar Biro, special rapporteur, "Situation of Human Rights in the Sudan," E/CN.4/1996/62, 20 February 1996, 13. According to an eye witness account

detailed to the rapporteur, one twelve-year-old girl in the group was raped before she was killed.

5. Biro, "Situation of Human Rights in the Sudan," 9.

6. Telephone interview of James Jacobson, president, Christian Solidarity International, USA, by Nina Shea, 8 November 1996.

7. Biro, "Situation of Human Rights in the Sudan," E/CN.4/1994/48, 1 February 1994, 17.

8. Testimony of Dr. Kevin Vigilante, representative, Puebla Institute, before the Subcommittee on International Relations and the Subcommittee on Africa, Committee on International Relations, U.S. House of Representatives, 13 March 1996.

9. Gilbert A. Lewthwaite and Gregory Kane, three-part series, *The Baltimore Sun,* 16–18 June 1996.

10. Testimony of the Baroness Cox, Christian Solidarity International, before the Subcommittee on International Relations and the Subcommittee on Africa, Committee on International Relations, U.S. House of Representatives, 13 March 1996.

PAKISTAN

11. Pakistani Legal Code, Sec. 295-C (1989), testimony of David F. Forte, professor of law, Cleveland State University, Cleveland-Marshall College of Law, before the Subcommittee on Near East and South Asia Affairs, Committee on Foreign Relations, U.S. Senate, 6 March 1996.

12. "Pakistan: Use and Abuse of the Blasphemy Laws," Amnesty International, ASA 33/08/94, July 1994, 1.

13. Ibid.

14. Statement of Nina Shea, director, Puebla Program on Religious Freedom, before Members' Briefing on Religious Persecution of the Congressional Human Rights Caucus, House of Representatives, 7 March 1996.

15. "Mobs Assault Punjabi Christians Amid Sectarian Clashes," News Network International, 6 July 1994.

16. David F. Forte, testimony, 6 March 1996.

SAUDI ARABIA

17. Statement of Nina Shea, director, Puebla Program on Religious Freedom, before Members' Briefing on Religious Persecution of the Congressional Human Rights Caucus, House of Representatives, 7 March 1996.

18. Testimony of Dr. Morton E. Winston, chair, Amnesty International Board of Directors, USA, before the Committee on International Relations, Subcommittee on International Operations and Human Rights, House of Representatives, 15 February 1996.

19. Ted Olsen, "Escaping Martyrdom in Saudi Arabia," *Christianity Today,* 15 July 1996, 57.

20. See Colin Powell, *My American Journey* (New York: Random House, 1995), 474.

EGYPT

21. Telephone interview of Rev. Keith Roderick by Nina Shea, 1 October 1996.

22. "Released Christian Prisoner Forbidden to Leave Egypt," News Network International, 8 September 1995.

23. "Amnesty Condemns Killing of Egyptian Christians," *Reuter,* 26 February 1996.

24. "Magazine Reports Rise in Murders of Christians," News Network International, 6 October 1996.

25. Ibid.

NIGERIA

26. "New Round of Violence Targets Christian Community in Kano," News Network International, July 14, 1995.

27. Richard Nyberg, "Fundamentalist Islam Seeps Down from North Africa," News Network International, 10 February 1995.

28. Testimony of Dr. Morton E. Winston, chair, Amnesty International Board of Directors, USA, before the Committee on International Relations, Subcommittee on International Operations and Human Rights, House of Representatives, 15 February 1996.

29. "Catholic Bishops Blast Military Rule, Repression," News Network International, 7 April 1995.

30. "New Round of Violence Targets Christian Community in Kano," News Network International, 14 July 1995.

31. "Christians on Alert Following Muslim Attacks," News Network International, 24 February 1995.

32. "Three Nigerian Christian Schools Closed for Not Teaching Islam," *Compass Direct,* 22 August 1996.

UZBEKISTAN

33. "Special Report: Central Asia: Religious Liberty Still a Casualty in East-West Crossroads," News Network International, 3 November 1995.

34. "New 'Secret Law' Restricts Religious Literature," News Network International, 19 May 1995.

35. Ibid.

36. Ibid.

CHAPTER 4 / PERSECUTION IN COMMUNIST COUNTRIES
CHINA

1. *China: Religious Persecution Persists,* Human Rights Watch/Asia, New York, N.Y., December 1975.

2. Ibid.

3. Ibid.

4. Testimony of Nina Shea, director, Puebla Program on Religious Freedom, Freedom House, hearings on "Most Favored Nation" status for China, before the Committee on International Relations, Subcommittee on International

Operations and Human Rights, U.S. House of Representatives, 18 June 1996.

5. Testimony of Nina Shea, director, Puebla Program on Religious Freedom, Freedom House, hearings on the persecution of Christians, before the Committee on International Relations, Subcommittee on International Operations and Human Rights, U.S. House of Representatives, 15 February 1996.

6. Telephone interview of David Stravers by Kim A. Lawton, 13 May 1996.

7. "China Premier Warns Religious to Obey Law," *Reuter,* 12 September 1996.

8. *China Focus,* the Princeton China Initiative, Princeton, N. J., 1 October 1996, 5.

9. "God's Country," *Far Eastern Economic Review,* 6 June 1996.

10. "Three Christians Beaten to Death in Fierce House Church Crackdown," *Compass Direct,* 27 June 1996.

11. "Appeal Letter to the Government of People's Republic of China from Bishop Su Zhimin, the Bishop of the Roman Catholic Diocese of Baoding, Heibei, China," translated and made available by the Cardinal Kung Foundation, 12 August 1996.

12. Steven Mufson, "China's Catholics Defy Ban on Church," *Washington Post,* 2 June 1995.

13. "Appeal Letter to the Government of People's Republic of China from Bishop Su Zhimin," 12 August 1996; Steven Mufson, "China Has More Catholics, More Repression," *Washington Post,* 6 October 1996.

14. "Urgent Action Appeal," Amnesty International, 14 August 1996.

15. See page 66, sentencing decision of reform through Labor Management Committee, the People's Government of Soochow, Province of Jiangsu, 4 January 1996, translated and made available by the Cardinal Kung Foundation.

16. Ibid.

17. "Appeal Letter to the Government of People's Republic of China from Bishop Su Zhimin," 12 August 1996.

18. Interview of American Bible missionary just returned from China by Nina Shea, Washington, D.C., 24 January 1996.

19. Ye Xiaowen, "On the Need to Conscientiously Implement 'Three Sentences' in Carrying Out Religion-related Work Well," *Renmin Ribao,* 9, as quoted in the Federal Broadcast Information Service, FBIS-CHI-96-072, 12 April 1996.

20. "New Crackdown on Religion in 1996," *China News and Church Report,* China Ministries International-Chinese Church Research Center, Hong Kong, 26 January 1996.

NORTH KOREA

21. Anne Himmelfarb, "Christianity in North Korea: Politics by Other Means," Research Association of the Puebla Institue, *America,* published by the Jesuits of the United States and Canada, 9 May 1992, 411.

22. Testimony of Nina Shea, director, Puebla Program on Religious Freedom, Freedom House, hearings on the persecution of Christians, before the Committee on International Relations, Subcommittee on International Operations and Human Rights, U.S. House of Representatives, 15 February 1996.

23. Ibid.

24. Andrew Wark, "Special Report: North Korean Christians Are Maintaining the Faith Amid Severe Communist Oppression," News Network International, 16 January 1995; "South Korean Missionary Reported Kidnapped by North Korea," News Network International," 11 August, 1995.

25. Statement of Nina Shea, director, Puebla Program on Religious Freedom, before Members' Briefing on Religious Persecution of the Congressional Human Rights Caucus, House of Representatives, 7 March 1996.

26. "North Korea Invites South Korean Catholic Priests to Pyongyang," News Network International, 24 February 1995.

VIETNAM

27. Testimony of Nina Shea, director, Puebla Program on Religious Freedom, Freedom House, hearings on the persecution of Christians, before the Committee on International Relations, Subcommittee on International Operations and Human Rights, U.S. House of Representatives, 15 February 1996.

28. Testimony of Tom White, USA director, Voice of the Martyrs, hearings on the persecution of Christians, before the Committee on International Relations, Subcommittee on International Operations and Human Rights, U.S. House of Representatives, 15 February 1996.

29. "Three Years, Six Months Prison for Vietnamese Christian," *An Open Letter,* the Voice of the Martyrs newsletter, Bartlesville, OK, March 1996.

30. *Vietnam: Free Market, Captive Conscience,* The Puebla Institute, Washington, D.C., September 1994.

31. Testimony of Nina Shea, director, Puebla Program on Religious Freedom, Freedom House, hearings on Vietnam, before the Subcommittee on International Operations and Human Rights and the Subcommittee on Asia and the Pacific, Committee on International Relations, U.S. House of Representatives, 8 November 1995.

32. Tom White testimony, 15 February 1996.

33. Nina Shea testimony, 15 February 1996.

34. "Vietnam Bishops Ask Prime Minister for Better Conditions for Church," *Asia Focus,* Union of Catholic Asian News, Bankod, 3 November 1996.

35. *Vietnam: Free Market, Captive Conscience,* September 1994.

36. Testimony of Rev. Tran Qui Thien, hearings on Vietnam, before the Subcommittee on International Operations and Human Rights and the Subcommittee on Asia and the Pacific, Committee on International Relations, U.S. House of Representatives, 8 November 1995.

37. Telephone interview with veteran Indochina expert who just returned from Vietnam by Kim A Lawton, 24 June 1996.

CUBA

38. Telephone interview of Pastor Eliezer Veguilla by Nina Shea, 24 October 1996.

39. Ibid.

40. Cuba: Castro's War on Religion, Puebla Institute, Washington, D.C., May 1991.

41. Ibid.

42. Shawn T. Malone, "Conflict, Coexistence, and Cooperation: Church-State Relations in Cuba," Cuba Briefing Paper Series, Center for Latin American Studies, Georgetown University, August 1996.

43. "Cuban Churches Face Increased Opposition," *Compass Direct*, 22 August 1996.

44. Ibid.

45. Malone, "Conflict, Coexistence, and Cooperation: Church-State Relations in Cuba," August 1996.

46. "A New Cuban Crisis," the Voice of the Martyrs newsletter, October 1996; "Third Cuban Christian Released from Prison," *Compass Direct*, 27 June 1996.

47. Testimony of Tom White, USA director, Voice of the Martyrs, hearings on the persecution of Christians, before the Committee on International Relations, Subcommittee on International Operations and Human Rights, U.S. House of Representatives, 15 February 1996.

48. *See, e.g.,* Malone, "Conflict, Coexistence, and Cooperation: Church-State Relations in Cuba," August 1996.

49. Ibid.

50. Ibid.

LAOS

51. "Tribal Christians Still Forced to Recant Faith," News Network International, 5 May 1995.

52. Ibid.

53. Report of the Mekong Prayer Fellowship, May to July 1996; Mekong Prayer Fellowship, P.O. Box 209, Sam San 10400 Thailand.

54. Telephone interview with veteran Indochina expert who just returned from Laos by Kim A Lawton, 24 June 1996.

55. Mekong Prayer Fellowship Report, May to July 1996.

56. Telephone interview, veteran Indochina expert, 24 June 1996.

57. Mekong Prayer Fellowship Report, May to July 1996.

CHAPTER 5 / CALL TO ACTION

1. Statement of Chuck Colson at Freedom House Conference on the "Global Persecution of Christians," 23 January 1996, Washington, D.C.

2. See appendix, "Statement of Conscience of the National Association of Evangelicals Concerning Worldwide Religious Persecution," 23 January 1996.

3. Ibid.

4. Ibid.

5. See appendix B, Denominational Resolutions and Letters of Support.

6. Pope John Paul's Annual Address to Diplomatic Corps, 13 January 1996, Vatican Information Service, 15 January 1996.

7. Testimony of Richard Land, president, Christian Life Commission of Southern Baptist Convention, before the Committee on International Relations, Subcommittee on International Operations and Human Rights, House of Representatives, 15 February 1996.

8. Stephen S. Rosenfeld, "Human Rights for Christians Too," *Washington Post*, 9 February 1996.

9. Ibid.

10. Ibid.

11. Land testimony, 15 February 1996.

12. Ibid.

13. Ibid.

14. Interview of Christopher Catherwood by Kim A. Lawton, Prague, Czech Republic, 6 May 1996.

15. Ibid.

16. Telephone interview of Michael Novak by Nina Shea, 10 October 1996.

17. Telephone interview of Diane Knippers by Nina Shea, 4 October 1996.

18. See appendix, "Statement of Conscience of the National Association of Evangelicals Concerning Worldwide Religious Persecution," 23 January 1996.

19. Land testimony, 15 February 1996.

20. See appendix C, Senate Concurrent Resolution 71, 17 September 1996.

21. See appendix C, House Resolution 515, 24 September 1996.

22. Land testimony, 15 February 1996.

23. Ibid.

24. Ibid.